THE OAU [AU] AND OAS IN REGIONAL CONFLICT MANAGEMENT: A COMPARATIVE ASSESSMENT

THE OAU [AU] AND OAS IN REGIONAL CONFLICT MANAGEMENT: A COMPARATIVE ASSESSMENT

T. A. Imobighe

Spectrum Books Limited
Ibadan
Abuja •Benin City •Lagos •Owerri

Spectrum titles can be purchased on line at
www.spectrumbooksonline.com

Published by
Spectrum Books Limited
Spectrum House
Ring Road
PMB 5612
Ibadan, Nigeria
e-mail: admin1@spectrumbooksonline.com

in association with
Safari Books (Export) Limited
1st Floor
17 Bond Street
St Helier
Jersey JE2 3NP
Channel Islands
United Kingdom

Europe and USA Distributor
African Books Collective Ltd
The Jam Factory
27 Park End Street
Oxford OX1, 1HU, UK

First published, 2003

ISBN: 978-029-374-4

Printed by Kenbim Press Ltd Ibadan

Dedication

THIS book is dedicated to the innocent victims of *conflicts,* and all those who labour to bring about a just and more peaceful world.

Contents

Preface

THE decision to carry out this study is motivated by the author's concern for the pervasive and apparently intractable nature of the numerous conflicts ravaging the global community, many of which have left a lot of destruction and human misery in their trial. Contrary to expectation, the end of the cold war has not resulted in any appreciable reduction in the incidents of violent conflicts across the globe. Rather than a drop in the world conflict profile, we are confounded by the spread of hostilities and violent conflicts, even to regions that had hitherto enjoyed some measure of stability. Thus, while it is correct to say that the cold war is over, we cannot say with confidence that we are any closer to winning the battle for global peace and security.

The destructiveness of these conflicts and the fact that many of them seem to persist put a question mark on the effectiveness of the efforts being made to manage them both at the global and regional levels. In other words, why have the conflict management efforts of such inter-governmental organisations (IGOs), like the United Nations at the global level, and the Organisation of African Unity (OAU) and the Organisation of American States (OAS) at the regional level, failed to yield the desired dividends? Perhaps, even more fundamental are such questions as – why have these conflicts persisted and, in many cases, intensified? What are the limitations in the efforts being made by IGOs to successfully manage these conflicts? What general conclusions can be drawn as to how best IGOs can play a more assertive and positive role in conflict management?

This study has made a bold attempt to find answers to these and other related questions by undertaking a comparative study of two IGOs with a relatively long history of practical involvement in conflict management. Most IGOs do not go beyond a casual reference in their charters to a commitment to pacific settlement of disputes and renunciation of the use of force in the settlement of disputes between their members. The choice of the OAU and OAS as case studies in this book emanated from the fact that the two organisations have gone beyond the conventional practice and have actually made elaborate institutional provisions for conflict management. Hence, it is felt that there can be no better way of getting at the root of the problem of conflict management by IGOs than by documenting the experiences of the two organisations and drawing relevant lessons from their successes and failures.

Using a model of an integrated conflict management system, which sees conflict management as a process comprising conflict prevention and peace promotion; conflict control and abatement; and conflict resolution, a more holistic picture of the conflict management activities of the OAU and OAS has been succinctly presented in this study. The analysis in his book covers ten case studies, five from each of the two regions studied; i.e. Africa and the Americas. From the ten case studies, it has been found that, like other IGOs, the two regional organisations exhibit a basic weakness in their approach to conflict management. This relates to their failure to see conflict management in its integrated form in which the activities of all the organs within each organisation are mutually reinforcing. Thus despite their relatively more elaborate machinery for conflict management, the OAU and OAS have each exhibited the same limitations suffered by other IGOs – a piecemeal approach, the resort to improvisation and a tendency to progress no further than mere control and abatement of conflicts.

In terms of overall score, the achievements of the OAU and OAS have been more in the area of conflict control and abatement than in the other two areas of conflict prevention and conflict resolution. While conflict abatement is an important element in a conflict management process, it cannot constitute a total success until the underlying issues in the conflict are effectively resolved to the mutual satisfaction of the parties. Admittedly, facilitating the process of serious negotiations between parties in conflict for the resolution of the fundamental issues involved in the conflict is a much more tedious task than conflict abatement. It is time-consuming and needs a lot of patience and dedication on the part of the mediator or facilitator. This is why ad hoc committees of foreign ministers and heads of state, often utilised by IGOs to manage conflicts, have not been quite effective; the reason being that they are hardly able to devote the time and energy needed to manage protracted conflicts due to other pressing demands on their time. It becomes imperative that if IGOs are to make any significant progress beyond conflict abatement, they should endeavour to avail themselves of the services of corps of mediators (formally or informally constituted) and with a mix of the relevant skills and expertise, who can devote their time and energy to engage the parties in conflict in the usually protracted negotiations to resolve their differences. This is where the OAU and the OAS need to strengthen their conflict management mechanisms in the manner suggested in this book.

The other area where the two organisations need to reinforce their conflict management mechanism relates to conflict prevention, where behavioural codes established by both organisations are necessary but not enough; and, therefore, need additional sinews in order to build mutual confidence and trust for a climate of peace to prevail within the two regions. On this score, whether the recent transformation of the OAU into AU can replicate the European Union (EU) magic is too early to tell. On the issue of IGOs' behavioural codes, this study presents an interesting contrast in the manner the OAU and OAS have tried to grapple with the problem of compliance. For the OAS, the main battle was with the challenge of taming an overbearing hegemon, the United States, while for the OAU, it was with the challenge of getting over its own obsession with an overriding desire for corporate unity.

OAU's Transformation into AU

As final touches were being put to the publication of this book, the member states of the Organisations of African Unity (OAU) signed a new memorandum transforming the organisation into what is now called the African Union (AU). The decision to adopt AU was reached on September 9, 1999 and formalised at the Durban Summit in South Africa on July 9, 2002. The AU is expected to carry on from where the OAU stopped, and bring about the full economic and political integration of African States. It is expected to fight poverty, eliminate human rights abuses, provide good governance, promote peace and security, and resolve conflicts within the African continent.

Although, besides the commitment to full economic and political integration, the goals of the AU are not fundamentally different from those of its predecessor, the organisation's metamorphosis from OAU to AU impinges on a major observation highlighted in this study. This relates to the observation that although the OAU and OAS have tried to encourage a climate of peace in their respective regions through the establishment of behavioural codes, they have failed to reinforce their codes of conduct with practical measures designed to build mutual trust and confidence; a key aspect of which should be the promotion of integrative activities within their respective regions. In other words, until now, both organisations were not seen to have aggressively pursued regional integration as an essential component of their conflict prevention and peace-building mechanism.

For instance, although the OAS countries had an early start on the road to regionalism, other regions have overtaken them, especially the EU, in terms of concretizing their efforts towards full integration. Similarly, although the OAU in 1991 signed the African Economic Community Treaty, little or no progress was made up to the time of its present transformation into AU, to mitigate the colonially-imposed mutual isolation of the African peoples within the continent. In other words, regional integration was yet to be made meaningful to the ordinary citizens of African states by facilitating free movement across state borders and promoting professional, social and economic contacts between them. In most cases, the enthusiasm, too often demonstrated at the signing of the affected instruments, was hardly sustained at the level of implementation.

A relevant question to ask at this point is what is in a change of name if the political will is not there to translate an organisation's commitment into practical reality. After all, as earlier noted, many of the commitments embodied in the AU instrument have always formed part of the agenda pursued by the OAU. So, will the present change of name automatically produce attitudinal change on the part of member states, for instance, in the provision of the needed resources to promote the full realisation of these commitments? Will it, for example, solve the unabating indebtedness of member states to the organisation – an indebtedness, which at the heart of its present transformation into AU, witnessed a situation whereby 45 member states out of 54 were in arrears in the payment of their subscriptions? Will it change the lukewarm attitude of member states to the "peace fund" set up to generate funds to service the organisation's conflict management activities? These are some of the relevant questions demanding AU's positive response, if it must overcome the limitations of its predecessor – limitations which have been succinctly documented in this study.

Admittedly, the AU instrument contains some new clauses meant to take care of some of the inhibitions suffered by the OAU. Some of these relate to the promotion of democracy and good governance, and the right of intervention in the internal affairs of member states in case of human rights abuses and genocide. Others relate to some of the structural changes meant to enhance the prompt intervention of the organisation in matters affecting the peace and security of the continent, such as the provision for a 15-nation Peace and Security Council, which was canvassed for unsuccessfully by some members of the OAU until now. However, while these are commendable innovations, the question still remains whether the organisation would be able to muster the necessary political will to implement the relevant provisions, as well as carry out the other institutional corrections proffered in this study to make the AU a better conflict manager than its predecessor.

Ambrose Alli University,
Ekpoma, Nigeria
June, 2002

T. A. Imobighe

Acknowledgements

THINKING of the people to whom I would like to express my appreciation for their support, suggestions and encouragement in making this study possible, has presented me with an endless list, which cannot be contained here. But, first, I must thank those who provided the means for this study.

My utmost appreciation goes to the organisers of the Fulbright programme, for the nine-month fellowship they granted me, which enabled me to work and interact with some of the leading experts in conflict management at the Institute of Conflict Analysis and Resolution, George Mason University, Fairfax, U.S.A. I cherish the interaction I had with the staff at the Institute, especially, John Burton, Chris Mitchell, Rich Rubenstein, Jim Laue and Joe Scimmecca.

Next, I will like to express my gratitude to the United States Institute of Peace for granting me a Peace Fellowship, which enabled me to complete this study. I benefited much from the interaction with the staff and colleagues on the Jennings Randolph Programme, and thank all of them for the various ways they have contributed to the success of this study. Of particular mention, is the tremendous assistance I got from Jocelyn Nieva and Blair G. Ewing, who worked with me during my one-year stay at the Institute. Also worthy of mention, is Alex George, a Distinguished Fellow on the Jennings Randolph Programme, for reading the entire manuscript and making useful suggestions. I should also like to thank Nigel Quinney of the Publications Unit for his editorial guidance and useful suggestions on the text of the manuscript.

I must not fail to mention my indebtedness to my friend and colleague, Professor Ibrahim A. Gambari, then Nigeria's Permanent Representative at the United Nations, whose hospitality and assistance facilitated the meetings I held with a number of officials of the United Nations and the International Peace Academy (IPA) in New York.

In addition, during the course of my research trips to the headquarters of the OAU and OAS, I made good use of their library facilities and had useful discussions with some members of staff, for which I am grateful. And to all the other individuals, too many to mention, with whom I interacted during the course of this study, I say a big thank you.

Finally, I will like to express my gratitude to my wife and children for the cordial environment they have always created at home, and the exemplary manner they have coped with my long absence from home during the course of this study.

In conclusion, I will like to add that I am solely responsible for the views expressed in this study and for whatever limitations it might have.

Introduction

CONFLICTS represent part of the dynamics of inter-state relations. But when conflicts become too frequent within a region, they divert attention from the more basic issues of development and the promotion of the aspirations of the people that are usually the primary concern of organised societies. In most cases, and especially where such conflicts escalate into open violence or wars, they actually consume substantial quantities of human and material-development resources. An inter-governmental organisation (IGO) within a conflict-ridden region can hardly ignore such conflicts and still function effectively. And if it must be involved, it must design a mechanism that allows conflicts to be dealt with promptly and efficiently, thereby freeing the organisation to concentrate on other issues. In short, an IGO has a basic interest in evolving measures that can help to prevent, control, and resolve conflicts among its members, thereby creating a climate of relative peace and harmony within which it can seek to meet the minimum expectations of its members.

The Organisation of African Unity (OAU), now African Union (AU) and the Organisation of American States (OAS) are two regional inter-governmental organisations that are committed to the promotion of the socio-cultural and economic welfare of their member-states. Both organisations, however, have been distracted from the pursuit of these objectives by numerous endemic and seemingly intractable conflicts within their respective regions. Precious time and energy have been dissipated in trying to settle these conflicts, the persistence of which has done nothing to promote the intra-regional harmony necessary to the effective pursuit of a collective development effort.

Recognising the need to order the relations among their members, both the OAU and the OAS have set up elaborate machinery for the peaceful resolution of conflicts within their regions. Whereas most regional IGOs are satisfied with references in their charters to the need for peaceful settlement of disputes among their members and the renunciation of the use of force, the OAU and OAS have taken conflict management beyond such conventional constitutional provisions. They have established not only rules to guide the behaviour of their members, but also a variety of institutions and formal processes for conflict management. And yet, despite these efforts, inter-state harmony remains elusive within the two regions.

The aim of this study is to examine the conflict management institutions, structures, and activities of the two organisations; and in the process, seek not merely explanations for their mixed past records but also suggestions as to how those performances might be improved in the future. By undertaking a comparative study of two regional organisations with a long record of involvement in the practical aspects of conflict management, it may be possible to arrive at some generally applicable conclusions regarding how inter-governmental regional bodies can play a more assertive and useful role in conflict management

A comparative assessment of the OAU and OAS in their conflict management roles has not, to the author's knowledge, been undertaken before. As such, this study may throw some new light not only on the two organisations under scrutiny, but also on conflict management in other regions of the world and on such far-reaching questions as the extent to which inter-state harmony can be maintained on the basis of general principles. The amenability of inter-state conflicts to formal processes of conflict management is another area this study is likely to throw some light.

Of course, this study does not claim to be comprehensive in terms of the range of conflicts that bedevil Africa and the Americas. In fact, the sheer number and diversity of the wars that have plagued the two continents in recent decades preclude an in-depth assessment of each conflict within a study of this modest size. Nor does this study claim to provide an exhaustive analysis of all the factors that contribute to both the promotion and the resolution of regional disputes. The emphasis here is on the organizational machinery created to deal with conflicts rather than on the political intricacies of those conflicts. This focus is dictated in part by the slim proportions of this study. In part, too, it reflects the author's desire to correct a neglect of organisational issues by scholars who have devoted far more attention to the political dimensions of regional conflicts. It is also the author's contention that many of the political difficulties that obstruct the OAU and OAS, as they seek to maintain or restore peace within their regions, are often compounded by organisational weaknesses. While political realities can militate against effective conflict management, inadequate conflict management machinery can equally militate against improving the political climate to permit meaningful negotiations to take place.

Readers should thus be aware of the parameters of this work. The author believes, however, that the variety of conflicts (five from each region) examined here is sufficient to indicate the main types of disputes with which the OAU and OAS have or have had to deal with. Similarly, the author trusts that the political background to each conflict is sketched in sufficient detail to convey a reasonable impression of the prevailing climate within which the attempt at conflict management was made. (Readers who wish to know more about the politics of a particular case are encouraged to consult the many excellent works that focus on that subject. Some of these have been sited in the relevant endnotes).

Chapter 1

The Concept and Practice of Conflict Management

THIS study is not, it should be emphasised, a theoretical one. The questions and issues addressed here are of practical import; affecting, in a very direct way, the well-being of the peoples of Africa and the Americas. At the same time, however, any comparative study, such as this, cannot completely rule out a consistent conceptual framework, if it is to marshal evidence and assess performances in an illuminating and even-handed fashion. In exploring and evaluating the conflict management records of the OAU and OAS, this study employs an analytical framework in which two closely interrelated concepts predominate: an integrated conflict management system, and the problem-solving approach. A brief discussion of these two elements is necessary.

Integrated Conflict Management System

Conflict management is concerned with the ways and means of controlling and harmonising conflictual relationships within an interaction process. In inter-state relations, conflict management concerns the way in which events, especially the stresses and strains in the relations between nations, are controlled to ensure some harmony between the parties concerned. If the conflictual relationship in human interaction is to be effectively controlled, it must be tackled at the roots. This means that efforts at conflict management must seek to eliminate the conditions that create an environment of conflict. In other words, one should not wait for conflict to erupt before taking action. This is the essence of the concept of an integrated conflict management system.

Conflict management in the integrated sense in which it is applied in this study represents a process embracing three types of activity: conflict prevention and/or peace promotion and consolidation; conflict control / abatement; and conflict resolution. Taken together, these three types of activity constitute what is here referred to as "the conflict management circle", represented below in figure 1.

Figure 1

Integrated Conflict Management Circle

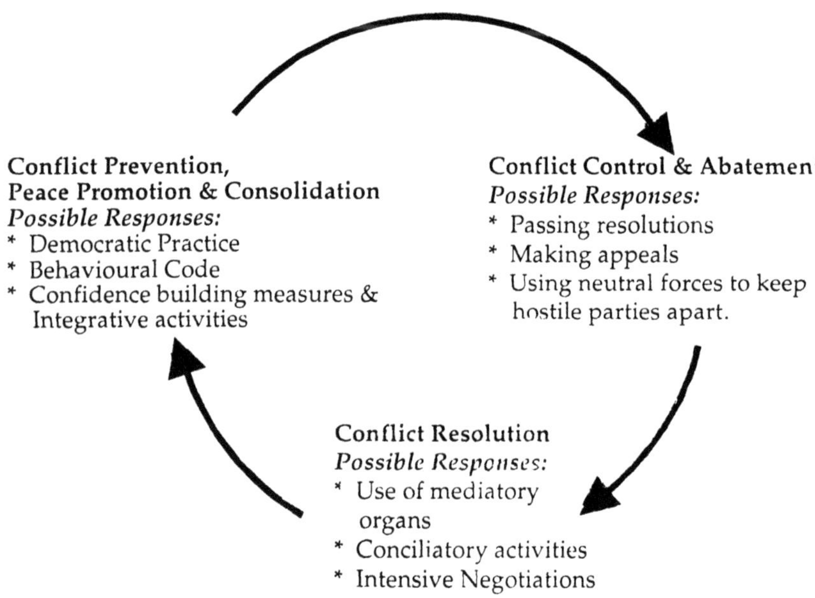

In recent years, some scholars have tended to treat conflict resolution as distinct from conflict management. They see conflict management as a means of preventing the escalation of a conflict rather than of resolving it.[1] This distinction seems only to apply, if one limits oneself to a purely strategic conception of conflict management in which the emphasis is on coercive techniques. If, however, the concept is conceived in its integrated form, conflict management can then represent a process in which the starting point is conflict prevention and/or peace promotion and consolidation through the elimination of the causes of friction and the creation of a propitious atmosphere for harmonious relationships. This presupposes the existence of a base point of relative peace and harmony in human or inter-state relationships. It is a point at which friction is kept at tolerable levels and conflict management is concerned with peace promotion and consolidation, as well as conflict prevention. If conflict, however, erupts for whatever reason, then conflict management moves to a second stage. At this second stage, the efforts of the conflict manager are directed toward trying to control and abate the conflict, to defusing tension in order to create a suitable climate for the third and final phase. This third phase involves the eventual resolution of the conflict through intensive negotiations to settle all the fundamental issues associated with the conflict. Once the affected issues are resolved, conflict management can then be said to have gone full circle, with the relationship between the parties having returned to a tolerable level of friction. The conflict manager is now concerned with promoting and consolidating peace by taking measures to prevent future conflicts.

Different types of conflict management responses or measures are applicable to each of the three stages. At the first stage, possible activities include democratic practice, the establishment of behavioural codes, the creation of confidence-building measures, and the development of integrative activities. Measures often used at the second stage include appealing to the parties in conflict to exercise restraint, passing resolutions on general principles or guidelines for settlement, and using neutral forces to keep the hostile parties apart. Possible responses at the third stage include various forms of conciliatory moves, intensive negotiations, and the use of mediatory organs.

The conflict management circle is particularly relevant to the logic of organisational conflict management. A regional IGO that takes on the role of a conflict manager should, apart from developing the necessary machinery for the peaceful resolution of conflicts within its region, first try to foster harmonious relationship among its members. For an IGO to neglect this comprehensive or integrated view of conflict management is to invite chaos and allow friction between members to overwhelm the organisation.

For the OAU and OAS, conflict management has a special significance in addition to the promotion of regional harmony. Latin America and, in particular, Africa have the greatest concentrations of underdeveloped nations of all the major regions of the world. Within the OAU, only Egypt and South Africa are capable of managing any significant emergency without resort to external sourcing of military hardware. Within the OAS, only the United States, Canada, Brazil and Argentina have the indigenous military hardware manufacturing capability to service a major war. Thus, most countries within both regions would find it more profitable to invest in conflict management techniques than to allow conflicts to escalate into wars in which they would have to waste their hard-earned foreign exchange on munitions.

One of the basic factors of insecurity and inter-state disharmony in the two regions has to do with underdevelopment; which has been compounded by the debt burden, diminishing levels of productivity experienced by a number of states, and by an inability to meet the basic needs of their peoples. Unnecessary investment in foreign-made military hardware is likely to worsen the situation still further, by draining scarce resources away from the development of domestic industries.

Approaches to Conflict Management

There are, of course, many different approaches to conflict management, each of which may have utility in particular circumstances. A great deal of scholarship has been devoted to analysing how and in what situations different approaches can be applied most effectively. This is not the place to conduct a review of this scholarly activity. Rather, given the fact that attention here is centred on the role of third parties in the management of conflicts, brief mention will be made of the variety of techniques available to the third-party manager. A fairly longer discussion will, however, deal with one of these techniques – the problem-solving approach – that is vital to the success of an integrated conflict management system. As subsequent chapters of this study will show the OAU and OAS have unfortunately tended to under-employ this latter approach.

Conflict management approaches can be classified in a number of ways. They can, for instance, be classified into two broad categories: firstly on the basis of the level of escalation at which the particular conflict is being managed...[2]. In this sense, one can distinguish between the "peaceful" and the "military" approaches. The trademarks of the peaceful approach are negotiation, verbal persuasion, use of inducements, denial of privileges, and subtle manipulation; short of the use of physical force,[3] while those of the military approach relate to the use of physical coercion. The use of physical force could be by a party to the conflict or by a third party, to promote one side's interests, impose a settlement, or create a situation in which diplomatic negotiations can occur.

Secondly, conflict management approaches can also be classified according to the status of the participants involved in the bargaining process. For example, a conflict could be managed through "negotiation", that is, direct bargaining by the parties involved in the conflict; or through "mediation" , that is, with the help of a third party.[4] Mediation can involve a wide range of activities, including fact finding, message carrying, providing good offices, and serving as an honest broker. Indeed, mediation can be used in a wider sense to include virtually all forms of third-party involvement in conflict management. Here, however, third-party involvement is classified into three types: the legal or judicial approach; the power-politics approach and the conciliatory approach.

The **judicial approach** relates to the management of conflict within a legal framework in which a third party is given, or assumes the responsibility of reaching an effective decision concerning the settlement or resolution of a conflict. Such a decision is usually reached in accordance with pre-existing societal or international norms; the decision may or may not be binding. Arbitration by the International Court of Justice (ICJ) is a good example of this approach. The main problem with the judicial approach is that it usually results in a win-lose outcome. As such, it does not always lead to the effective resolution of a particular conflict, and parties to a conflict that are not favoured by the decision frequently choose to ignore it. Fear of being adversely affected by judicial settlement often makes parties reluctant to refer their conflicts to a legal process. As this study shows, these problems have frequently undermined the effectiveness of the elaborate legal frameworks created by the OAU and OAS to manage conflicts within their regions.

In the **power-politics approach**, third parties seek to manage conflicts out of a concern with their own broader strategic interests rather than with the interests of the parties to the conflict. For instance, throughout the Cold War, the superpowers managed conflicts largely on the basis of how the outcomes might affect the East-West strategic balance. Arms balancing (keeping both sides at roughly equal levels of military strength while reaping economic rewards for arms-exporting nations) and the use of threats, blackmail, and coercive physical intervention are common techniques employed in the power-politics approach. As might be expected, this approach rarely addresses the underlying causes of a conflict, and thus tends to produce either win-lose outcomes or, at best, postpone future hostilities. The only type of coercive physical intervention not confined within the straightjacket of the power politics approach is the use of peacekeeping forces, especially by IGOs, to impose or maintain a cease-fire so that efforts toward a diplomatic solution can be pursued.

The **conciliatory approach** involves a process in which the third party tries to bring the parties in conflict to agreement through improving communications between them, helping to interpret the issues that divide them, and exploring avenues toward a peaceful settlement. The essence of the conciliatory approach is to facilitate contact between the parties and provide them with an opportunity for face-to-face negotiation; thereby enabling them to appreciate each other's fears and concerns and to seek mutual understanding at the negotiating table. Intractable conflicts especially those involving deep emotions, necessarily require the systematic replacement of negative feelings and perceptions with positive ones and thereby helps the parties in conflict discover some mutuality of interests which could be capitalised on for the resolution of the conflict in question.

Among the conflict management methods that can be

grouped under the conciliatory approach are appeasement, need satisfaction, and problem solving. These three management techniques are closely related; indeed, all could be regarded as facets of problem-solving methodology. Appeasement is based on the proposition that conflicts usually become intractable and escalate into wars because of the failure to redress legitimate grievances. Of course, determining legitimate grievances is no easy task, and appeasement is (as Hitler demonstrated) open to abuse. Yet, despite its poor reputation, one cannot but agree with Herman Kahn that the slogan: "appeasement never pays", is misleading, and that there are many cases where accommodation and flexibility have not only prevented war but also led to détente, entente, and friendship.[5]

Human need satisfaction, as a conflict management technique, is not very different from appeasement. According to John Burton, the technique's leading exponent, human beings have certain needs that are "human and not malleable," and that must be satisfied if there is to be development and conforming behaviour.[6] Any policy that neglects human needs thus cannot but generate protest behaviour and conflict.

Like the theory of appeasement, human needs theory seeks to get at the root of conflict, and to explore and respond to the reasons for protest and deviant behaviour that tend to generate conflict. However, human need theory also suffers from a similar problem to that faced by appeasement theory, namely, how to determine the irreducible minimum of the needs that must be satisfied to ensure societal harmony. Just as it is difficult to agree on what constitute legitimate grievances, it is not easy to determine the irreducible minimum of needs to be satisfied. Moreover, the satisfaction of one need merely leads to the assertion of another. Like appeasement, human need theory is a prey to the insatiability of the human appetite. Thus, for the theory to be of any practical value, there is always need to reach an agreement on the irreducible minimum of needs to be satisfied. Not surprisingly, such agreement is hard to obtain.

Appeasement and human need satisfaction theories are closely connected with problem-solving theory. Problem solving, as a conflict management technique, seeks to get at the root of conflict through an analytical process. It assumes that conflict is generally a response to frustrated needs. Hence, to resolve a conflict, one must first seek to identify the frustrated needs to be satisfied, and then work out the various options available for their satisfaction so as to arrive at some mutuality of interests between the parties, which they can explore to resolve the conflict. The problem-solving technique thus provides the opportunity for exploring "win-win" outcomes.[7]

To talk of problem solving without addressing the source of the problem is meaningless. Therefore, problem solving at the level of intra-state and inter-state relations must also seek to alter the conditions that breed friction and unrest in societal relations. It is in this sense that problem solving approach provides a far greater opportunity than do other conflict management methods for a comprehensive analysis of the issues involved in a conflict. Because it does not encourage fixed positions or notions, it implies throwing all the cards on the table. Hence, it makes the parties to a conflict more attuned to each other's interests, needs, fears and concerns; it therefore has a greater chance of leading them to a mutually acceptable agreement.

Among the techniques that have been developed for realising the objectives of the problem-solving approach are problem solving workshops, two-track or multi-track diplomacy, satisfaction of needs, redressing grievances, interests harmonisation, and third-party facilitation. There is no need for a detailed discussion of these techniques here. This is because many of them have been adequately covered in existing literature.[8] What needs to be emphasised is that seeing conflict management within the context of problem solving predisposes the conflict manager toward the resolution of the fundamental issues involved in conflict. However, the technique or techniques the conflict manager actually uses greatly depends on the circumstances surrounding the particular conflict.

What should also be emphasised is that conflict resolution is usually the most difficult of the three stages within the conflict management circle. Results do not come easily. At times, political circumstances may not be conducive to meaningful negotiations. The degree of bitterness among the key actors in a conflict might make it almost impossible to persuade them to sit at the negotiating table. The actors may wish, for domestic political reasons, to continue the conflict. Nonetheless, all these situations only underline the need for an IGO to create and maintain a mediating body able to devote the time and energy necessary to persuade the recalcitrant parties to negotiate.

Application of the problem-solving approach to conflict management by a third party, irrespective of the techniques used, entails a lot of work and skill. To widen the horizons of the parties in conflict and encourage them to shift from their rigid positions, the third-party mediator must be prepared to carry out an elaborate analysis of the conflict and bring into focus the salient issues involved. The fears and concerns of the parties, the values and goals they pursue, the various options available for the realization of these values and goals; and the costs of applying these options must be well articulated.

Obviously, this type of analysis is not the type to expect at conference summits; neither can an enduring solution to a deep-rooted conflict be obtained through conference resolutions, which are among the most common conflict management methods used by IGOs. However, this is not to say that IGOs cannot employ or facilitate the problem-solving approach. In actual fact, IGOs could serve, and indeed have served, as useful instruments of the problem-solving approach, provided appropriate and effective structures are in place. Two suggestions stand out from the brief assessment of the various approaches to conflict management here, if an IGO is to employ the problem-solving techniques effectively in its conflict management activities. First, it must be prepared to effect some structural changes and, second, it must be ready to mitigate its rigid adherence to the traditional methods exemplified by conference diplomacy and summit resolutions.

What structural changes are necessary as far as the OAU and OAS are concerned will become clearer from an examination of their conflict management machinery, activities and records. In the subsequent chapters of this study, the extent to which the OAU and OAS applied the problem-solving technique, as well as the extent to which this influenced their effectiveness as conflict managers, is analysed. As will be seen, much of the success and a great deal of the failure of the two organisations in managing conflicts can be traced to their use or neglect of the problem-solving approach.

Notes

1. John W. Burton, *Resolving Deep-rooted Conflict: A Handbook* (Lanham, Md. New York, and London: University Press of America, 1987), p.8; John W. Burton, *Conflict: Resolution and Provention* (New York: St. Martin's Press, 1990), p. 3; and William I. Zartman, *Ripe for Resolution: Conflict and Intervention in Africa.* (New York: O.U.P., 1985).

2. Here, it might be wise to acknowledge the important debate about the exact moment at which third-party intervention should be made. William Zartman's theory of the "mutual, hurting stalemate" (see Zartman, *Ripe for Resolution*, pp. 7 & 236) has justly received much attention. Although it may be noted that this concept is applicable only to highly escalated conflicts involving open hostilities; a wider application of the theory would otherwise amount to discouraging third-party mediation at lower levels of escalation. For the purpose of effective management of conflict at those lower levels, Kenneth Boulding's postulation of "catching the conflict young" (see Kenneth Boulding, *Conflict and Defence: A General Theory*, [New York and London: Harper & Row, 1962], p. 325), seems more helpful. No general rule seems to apply regarding the most propitious moment for the success of third-party intervention; everything depends on the level of escalation at which such intervention is being contemplated.

3. Alexander George's concept of "coercive diplomacy" may be regarded as the limit of this peaceful approach to crisis bargaining. See, for example, Alexander George, *Forceful Persuasion: Coercive Diplomacy as an Alternative to War* (Washington, D.C: United States Institute of Peace Press, 1992).

4. The concepts of negotiation and mediation have been extensively treated in scholarly literature. See, among others, Saadia Touval and William I. Zartman, eds., *International Mediation in Theory and Practice* (Washington D.C,: Westview Press for SAIS, 1985); and K. Webb and C.R Mitchell, eds., *New Approaches to International Mediation* (New York: Greenwood Press, 1988). See also D. Pruitt, *Negotiation Behaviour* (New York: Academic Press, 1981); and K. Kressel and D.G. Pruitt, eds., *Mediation Research* (San Francisco: Jossey Bass, 1989).

5. Harman Kahn, *On Escalation: Metaphors and Scenarios* (London: Pall Mall Press, 1965), p. 224.

6. John W. Burton, *On the Need for Conflict Prevention*, Occasional Paper 1 (Centre for Conflict Analysis and Resolution, George Mason University: Fairfax, VA., September 1989), pp. 7-8. See also, in addition to his works cited above, Burton's *Deviance, Terrorism and War* (New York: St. Martin's Press, 1979); and *Global Conflict* (Sussex England: Wheatsheaf, 1984).

7. The idea of a "win-win" outcome has been criticised by some scholars as unrealistic. John Keltner, for instance, has argued that the idea of anyone winning at the bargaining table creates the inevitability of someone losing, and thus Keltner favours talking about mutual agreement rather than win-win. See John W. Keltner *Mediation: Toward a Civilised System of Dispute Resolution* (Urbana, III: Eric & Sea Publications, 1987), pp. 5-6.

   Keltner's argument is reasonable. However, the concept of winning in conflict management should not be seen in terms of one side winning everything or both sides winning the same thing. Rather, it is meant to indicate a mutually satisfactory outcome for the parties to a conflict – what Dean Pruitt would regard as an "integrative solution". See Dean Pruitt, "Collective Approaches to Negotiation," in Dennis Sandole and Ingrid Sandole-Staroste, eds., *Conflict Management and Problem-solving: Interpersonal to International*

Applications (New York: New York University Press, 1987), p. 75.

8. C. R. Mitchell, *Peacemaking and the Consultant's Role* (London: Gower, 1981); R.J. Fisher, "The Third Party Consultant: A Method for the Study and Resolution of Conflict," *Journal of Conflict Resolution* 16, No. 1 (1972); pp. 67-94; and J. W. Macdonald and D. B. Bendahmane, *Conflict Resolution: Track Two Diplomacy* (Washington, D.C. Foreign Service Institute 1987). See also J.W. Macdonald and L. Diamond, *Multi-track Diplomacy: A System Guide and Analysis* (Grinnell, Iowa State: Iowa Peace Institute, 1991); and C.R. Mitchell, "Necessitous Man and Conflict Resolution: More Basic Questions About Basic Needs," in J. W. Burton, ed., *Conflict: Human Needs Theory* (New York: St. Martin's Press, 1990).

Chapter 2

An Overview of Conflict Management by IGOs (Regional and Global)

Regionalism in Today's World

STATES are increasingly compelled to reconcile themselves to the realities of the international system. Even though they still try to guard their sovereignty as jealously as possibly, it is apparent that the era of rigid adherence to sovereignty by States is rapidly passing away. States are growing increasingly aware of their need to cooperate in the exploitation and utilisation of world resources for the benefit of all the members of the international community. With the dawn of the 21st century, the concept of a global village has virtually become a reality, thanks to the revolution in communication and information technology and the widening and deepening impact of international economic inter-dependence. Consequently, it has become obvious that States need one another to realise and maximise their individual interests, and that the individual well-being of each member of the international community enhances the health and vitality of the entire global system.

Admittedly, the opportunities offered by the inter-dependence of nation-states in the present global system have not been fully exploited to satisfy the needs of all the members of the international community. Nonetheless, it is encouraging to note that states are breaking out from their sovereign shells and reaching out to one another. New regional and sub-regional groupings are being formed while old ones are being consolidated.

Hardly has any area of the globe been left untouched by the rising tide of regionalism. In Africa, for instance, there is the OAU; in the Americas, the OAS; and in Europe, the Council of Europe and the Commission on Security and Co-operation in Europe (CSCE). There are also many subregional groupings throughout the world. In Asia, for example, there are the South Asian Association for Regional Co-operation (SAARC) and the Association of South East Asian Nations (ASEAN), among others; and in the Middle East, organisations such as the League of Arab States exist. Apart from these regional and subregional organisations, there are the global groupings, most notably the United Nations Organisation, commonly referred to simply as the United Nations. The situation is such that it is difficult to find an independent State, except when it is deliberately barred by some special sanctions or circumstances, that does not belong to, at least, one regional IGO, in addition to its membership in the United Nations.

Perhaps the most distinctive feature of the pattern of modern regional groupings is not so much a question of their number and spread as to their purpose. Whereas earlier international groupings (both during the cold war and before) were mainly competitive alliance systems, which were confrontational in outlook, most present-day organisations are generally development-oriented and more co-operative in nature than confrontational. Although some relics of confrontational security groupings still exist, their continuing relevance has become increasingly open to question since the end of the cold war.

A major problem that afflicted these earlier regional groupings, and which often accounted for their early demise, was that most of them were designed essentially as competitive alliance systems. Besides, the method of conflict management for which they were fully equipped was the power politics approach, an approach that gave a leading role to coercive processes and that, as a consequence, frequently resulted in open military confrontations and wars. Once the competitive hostile relationship between two opposing alliance systems degenerated into a war, those systems lost their credibility as security providers. Almost invariably, they faded out of existence with the conclusion of the war as their members searched for new coalitions. The dissolution after World War I of both the Triple Entente and the Triple Alliance systems, and the emergence of the League of Nations is a case in point.

An important lesson to learn from this historical experience is that contemporary regional IGOs, if for no other reason, at least, for the sake of their own survival, must find effective ways of managing conflicts within the areas they cover. Only within a non-confrontational atmosphere can these organisations mobilise the collective will and resources of their members to promote the common interests that brought the members together in the first place.

The present international atmosphere would seem to be propitious for the development of effective techniques of conflict management by IGOs. The world is moving away from an era of confrontational alliances and coalition toward an era of functional co-operation, which is more conducive to the exploitation of mutually beneficial methods of conflict management. In this new era, states are becoming ever more attracted to functional and development-oriented organisations that are committed to the co-prosperity of their members. Such organisations would seem to be well suited to exploit the opportunities offered by conflict management techniques such as problem solving and conciliation.

In practice, however, few IGOs have become directly involved in conflict management. Many organisations look up to the United Nations rather than to themselves to act in this area, preferring to rely on the existing facilities and expertise of the world organisation rather than undertake the costly and often divisive business of conflict management themselves. Neither SAARC nor ASEAN, for example, has yet to involve itself directly in conflict management. Such action as has occurred in their regions tends to have been undertaken either by the United Nations or by countries acting individually (as in the case of India's intervention in Sri Lanka in 1987). In fact, it was not until at their July 2000 Summit, that any serious discussion was undertaken by ASEAN members on the modalities for intervention in crisis and human rights issues affecting its members. Other organisations have had only a more or less casual involvement in conflict management. For example, the Commonwealth of Nations lacks any structured mechanism for promoting or restoring peace, but merely responds to conflicts on an ad hoc basis. Even the Economic Community of West African States (ECOWAS), which was deeply involved in the peace efforts in Liberia from August 1990 to August 1997, lacked any approved institutional mechanism for servicing peace-keeping or monitoring peace support operations at the time it intervened in Liberia.

As for those organisations that do possess formal commitments to, and instruments for the promotion, maintenance, and restoration of peaceful relations among their members, their records show an uneven level of activity and success at the different stages within the conflict management circle. There is no space here to embark on a detailed examination of the activities of each of these organisations. Nonetheless, short overviews of two organisations (the United Nations and the League of Arab States), will help to illustrate some common strengths and weaknesses in conflict management by regional IGOs. Although the UN and the Arab League are quite different in most respects, they both suffer from some of the same short-comings in their attempts at dealing with disputes among their members.

The United Nations

Of the three stages within the conflict management circle, the United Nations has been most active at the stage of conflict control. In its efforts to abate, contain, and isolate violent disputes that endanger international peace and security, the organisation has frequently employed peace-keeping or observer forces. The main motive has been to separate combatants, maintain cease-fire, and monitor the implementation of agreements.[1] Indeed, due to its relative effectiveness in this area, the UN conflict management role has become virtually synonymous with peace-keeping. This peace-keeping bias is not unconnected with the fact that the United Nations was conceived first and foremost as a collective security organ, more attuned to coercive enforcement than to conflict management activities per se. Due to its inability to carry out the type of enforcement action envisaged in its Charter (a failing that has owed much to the readiness of one or some of the permanent members of the Security Council to veto such action), the United Nations has restricted itself to the less controversial role of peace-keeping. The East-West ideological confrontation after World War II, known as the cold war, created obstacles against the achievement of consensus at the Security Council on enforcement action, especially where the culprit is an ally or friend of any of the five permanent members.

Even in the area of peace-keeping however, the United Nations has encountered many difficulties, including costly delays in mobilising peace-keeping forces, imprecise mandates, apparently interminable missions, and serious logistical deficiencies. Logistic problems have also played a large role in undercutting the United Nations' authority over the only two enforcement operations it has formally undertaken. In the cases of UN action on the Korean Peninsula in the early 1950s and in the Gulf in 1991, control over military operations was exercised, not by the United Nations but by the United States, which in both instances took the initiative to act. It also supplied most of the troops and materials.

The United Nations has made some efforts with respect to the first stage within the conflict management circle; conflict prevention and peace promotion. Within its Charter and various other official instruments, the organisation has developed and enunciated what can be regarded as rules of behaviour to guide member states in their relations with one another. The main problem with the organisation's efforts in this area is that of compliance by member states. Very often, member states disregard those UN rules, principles, and decisions that seem to threaten their national interests, frequently justifying their non-compliance by referring to their sovereign independence. Although the United Nations can resort to sanctions to ensure compliance, the reckless use of the veto in the Security Council has generally made sanctions difficult to impose and enforce. For most practical purposes, then, the world body must rely on moral force to persuade its members to tow the line. Needless to say, moral force is often ineffective. The degree to which member states respond to such pressure depends greatly on the extent to which the United Nations has been responsive to their aspirations and needs. It is important to note that international co-operation or State commitment to the regulation of international norms is always a political decision and needs a political will to sustain. If the political will is absent, an organisation becomes ineffective no matter how forthright its stated goals and how just the principles enshrined in its charter may be.

It is at the third level of activity – the actual resolution of conflicts – that the United Nations has been least effective. Although Article 33 of the UN Charter enjoins "the parties to any dispute" to first of all "seek a solution by negotiation, mediation, conciliation, arbitration, judicial settlement, resort to regional agencies or arrangements, or other peaceful means," the parties are apparently meant to do so outside the UN structure. Only when they are unable to settle their conflicts through their own efforts can they refer their conflict to the Security Council, which can "decide to recommend such terms of pacific settlement as it may consider appropriate" (Article 37), including referring legal disputes to the International Court of Justice (ICJ).

The UN structure contains no conflict management organ to take the countries in dispute through the charter's list of methods of peaceful settlement (save for the ICJ's role in judicial settlements and arbitration). Thus, the best that can be expected from the arrangement is a process of conference-type hearings that leads to the passage of an innocuous resolution. Even such a resolution often falls victim to the veto power of the permanent members of the Security Council. Summit hearings and conference resolutions are not, to put it mildly, the best methods for dealing with the fundamental issues underlying a conflict. Resolving those issues requires bringing the parties together to engage in serious negotiation and explore mutually acceptable solutions; to do this, an IGO needs an effective mediatory organ that can act as a facilitator in the resolution of conflicts among its member states. This, the United Nations lacks. Due to the organisation's inability to complete the conflict management circle, a number of UN peace-keeping operations have continued for decades, with the opposing sides remaining entrenched in seemingly immutable hostility. Usually, only in those situations where concerned third parties, including the UN Secretary General, have taken the initiative to bring the parties to serious negotiations have peace-keeping missions ended successfully.

If the United Nations is to fill the gap caused by the absence of a mediatory organ, two possible options present themselves.

First, the office of the Secretary General can establish a small cell of mediators to act as facilitators in the resolution of conflicts through sustained mediatory efforts, especially, after the world body has been able to abate hostilities through the deployment of its peace-keeping forces or in some other ways. The mediators could also take timely action to "catch conflicts young," bringing parties in conflict together at an early stage before the conflict escalates into violence. A second option for the world body might be to rely on the services of regional organisations that possess reliable conflict management mechanisms. Some pockets of ad hoc co-operation, inspired by the initiative of leaders of both the United Nations and some regional entities, already exist between the United Nations and regional organisations. Examples of such collaboration include joint UN-OAU operations in Namibia, Western Sahara, and South Africa; as well as joint action, albeit of a much more limited kind, by the United Nations and the OAS in respect of Haiti, Nicaragua, and El Salvador. It may be noted that Articles 52 and 53 of the UN Charter assign explicit roles for regional organisations in the peaceful settlement of disputes between UN member states and in enforcement actions. It is worth remarking that the former UN Secretary General, Boutros-Ghali, in his 1992 report, *An Agenda for Peace,* advocated the need for a more systematic co-operation between the world body and regional organisations.[2] However, as the following discussion of the League of Arab Nations indicates, whether or not regional and sub-regional organisations can actually fulfil the roles that the UN Charter envisages, is open to question.

The League of Arab Nations

The League of Arab Nations was created to perform a variety of functions, including strengthening relations among its member states, co-ordinating their policies, to safeguarding their independence and sovereignty, and fostering close co-operation on economic, financial, cultural and other matters. The league is also expected to act as a mediator in disputes between its members or between its members and non-member states. The League Council, comprising representatives of member states, is the policy-making organ of the Arab League. It is charged with the task of realising all the objectives of the organisation, as well as supervising the execution of all its plans. It is also charged with the responsibility of mediating in all disputes, with a view to reconciling the parties involved. The jurisdiction of the Council is, however, limited to disputes which both parties consent to bring before it, and which do not – as Article 5 of the Pact of the League of Arab States declares – "concern a state's independence, sovereignty, or territorial integrity." These provisions tend to rule almost all substantive disputes out of the jurisdiction of the League Council.

The Arab League has no effective institutional mechanism for the peaceful resolution of conflicts other than the League Council, where conference-type diplomacy is the usual mode of response. The limitations in trying to settle conflicts on the basis of conference resolutions are all too apparent. They usually end up with palliative measures or appeals, which rarely touch on the fundamental issues behind the conflict. The "Arab Tribunal of Arbitration" mentioned in the pact, which would have served as part of the organisation's mechanism for conflict management, has so far failed to materialise. As one scholar has remarked, "the lack of formal machinery for the settlement of disputes, along with the sweeping restrictions on the jurisdiction of the League Council, undoubtedly contribute to the apparent inability of the Arab States to agree among themselves, while the Arab League remains impotent."[3]

Lacking a mediatory organ equipped to bring adversaries to the negotiating table in the search for a lasting settlement, the Arab League has had to rely on ad hoc arrangements in which the office of its secretary-general has played a prominent role. At times, individual member states or groups of member states have tried to reconcile the parties in conflict. In those conflicts where the League has played a role, its action has not gone beyond helping to negotiate a cessation of hostilities and deploying peace-keeping or observer forces. Examples include the Kuwait-Iraq conflict in 1961, the civil strife in Oman from 1970 to 1976, the conflict between North and South Yemen in 1972, and the Lebanese civil strife in 1975 and 1976. Because the fundamental issues have usually been left unresolved, a number of these conflicts have flared up intermittently.

In most other regional conflicts, the League's role has been relatively insignificant, and changed circumstances rather than effective mediation have led to the discontinuation of hostilities. For instance, the Syria-Iraq conflict of 1949 lapsed with the overthrow of Syrian President Husni Za'im, and the tension between Jordan and Syria over the latter's support of Jordanian dissidents ended with the Jordanians' decisive defeat of the dissidents in 1970. Also the Arab League could not do much in the territorial dispute between Iraq and Kuwait, which led to the attempted annexation of the latter by the former. But for the intervention of the United States and her allies through the effective use of the instrumentality of the UN, that aggression could not have been reversed.

As a result of the League's inability to effectively deal with these conflicts, a number of them have found their way to the United Nations, where many have been contained or abated, but not resolved, by the deployment of UN peace-keeping forces. Virtually all the conflicts between Arab League members and non-members have been referred to the world body or handled by some interested third-party outside the League. Among the last category of conflicts are those between Tunisia and France (1948 and 1961); Syria and Turkey (1957); the Algerian independence struggle against France (1948-1962); Egypt versus Israel, Britain, and France (1956); the Arab-Israel conflict (1948, 1967 and 1973); and the Iran-Iraq War (1980-1988).

Judged in terms of all three stages within the conflict management circle, the Arab League is clearly a relatively weak conflict manager. First, in the area of conflict prevention, peace promotion, and peace consolidation, the Pact of the League failed to provide a comprehensive code to order the behaviour of member states. Only two clauses concern members' behaviour, one prohibiting the use of force, the other urging members to respect the systems of government of other member states. Even though establishing basic rules of conduct does not always guarantee their observance by the affected states, such rules of conduct do have a way of checking excessive unilateralism by members of an IGO. States will no doubt, always act in accordance with their national interest, but in doing so, they also try to guard against accusations of disregarding the agreed norms of organisations to which they belong.

The Arab League has made only limited progress in promoting regional integration and co-operation. Its programmes in these areas have focused on interaction among Arab professionals in the socio-cultural, educational, and, to a lesser degree, economic fields. In the political sphere, mutual trust, especially among the ruling elite, is relatively low because of their pronounced concern for regime security and the mutual expectation of threat through support of dissidents by neighbouring states. Of course, the League cannot by itself overcome this deeply rooted and multi-faceted distrust. However, were the League able to capitalise on the present level of professional interaction with a rapid move toward greater integration, the prospects for greater harmony and understanding would improve.

At the stage of conflict control, the League has recorded some success, helping to stop hostilities and deploying peace-keeping or observer forces to supervise the disengagement of hostile forces. It is instructive to note that despite the lack of provision in the instrument setting up the League for the peaceful settlement of conflicts, there is an elaborate provision, under a separate treaty (the 1950 Joint Defence and Economic Co-operation Treaty), for defence and regional security. This helps to explain the relative ease with which the organisation has been able to mobilise peace-keeping or observer forces such as in Iraq-Kuwait border in 1961-1963, Oman in 1970-1979 and Lebanon in 1975-1976. Unfortunately, however, there is no such elaborate and effective mechanism for the harder task of conflict resolution.

The CSCE Arrangement

The Conference on Security and Co-operation in Europe (CSCE) is a bold undertaking in Europe, which brings together former cold war enemies (the Warsaw Pact and NATO countries) towards a common security endeavour. Under the CSCE arrangement, these countries agreed on a framework for a pan-European security, which encompasses a number of confidence-building measures and the setting up of a mechanism for conflict management. With what is already in place under the CSCE process, there are a few encouraging signs that some of the inherent weaknesses in the conflict management structures of the United Nations and Arab League as identified above may have been taken into consideration by the CSCE member states in their efforts to create a more effective regional mechanism for conflict management in Europe.

At their meetings in Valletta and Berlin in 1991, members of the CSCE designed a mechanism for the peaceful settlement of disputes that includes a mediatory organ. Under the arrangement, a "register of mechanism candidates" is to be maintained at the office of the Director of the Centre for the Prevention of Conflicts (CPC) in Vienna. Each CSCE member state is expected to submit the names of four qualified persons to be included in the register, from which one or more persons could be selected to serve as third parties for the resolution of conflicts brought before the CSCE. The CSCE arrangement is intended to be informal and flexible. Essentially, the small group of mediators, known as the "mechanism", is expected to facilitate the resolution of disputes by the parties themselves.

If the CSCE countries succeed in creating an effective mediatory organ, it will be a significant improvement on the Arab League and UN arrangements. If in addition, the North Atlantic Treaty Organisation (NATO) can be reorganised to form the peace keeping/enforcement nucleus of the CSCE arrangement, then all the vital processes of our projected integrated conflict management system would have been covered. It is at present too early to determine how the suggested NATO transformation would take place; and hence the effectiveness of this pan-European security arrangement. The plan to expand NATO to include Eastern European countries formerly under the Soviet orbit has not received the blessing of Russia. The latter's preference is the dissolution of NATO in favour of an entirely new pan-European security system that would embrace both East and West European countries within the framework of the CSCE. The feeling is that with the dissolution of the Warsaw Pact, retaining NATO, its rival body, would amount to unnecessary perpetuation of the relics of the cold war. Despite Russian opposition, the United

States and its Western allies are pressing on with the proposed enlargement of NATO with a redefined mission. Reorganising NATO for a peace-keeping/enforcement role within the CSCE conflict management arrangement can hardly be done without providing a role for Russia.

If the CSCE arrangement is to work satisfactorily, all these grey areas must be resolved. The delay in operationalising its mechanism prevented the CSCE from playing any tangible role in the management of the bloody imbroglio that ravaged the former Yugoslavia. This led to the shifting of the stage of managing the conflict to the United Nations. The United States, especially since 1995, has played the leading role in the diplomatic efforts to resolve the conflict. To keep the diplomatic momentum on course, the threat, and at times actual use, of military strikes by NATO forces have been resorted to. These have helped in mitigating the frequent manifestation of aggressive moves by the parties involved in the conflict. It is the deployment of NATO peace-keeping forces in Bosnia and Kosovo that has brought about uneasy peace in the region. The fact that NATO countries were able to work out some form of collaboration with Russia during the operations in Kosovo is an indication that some form of accommodation is possible.

If in the coming years the CSCE is able to establish a well-organised and well-trained body of mediators, as well as work out a form of accommodation with NATO, the CSCE should be relatively well placed to help sustain negotiations between adversaries until mutually acceptable settlement can be reached. Conflicts in Europe might then stand a much greater chance of being not only contained but also resolved.

It is important to emphasise that even the best institutional arrangement will not make the path toward conflict resolution less tortuous, either in Europe or elsewhere. Nor will the existence of a carefully designed mediatory organ ever ensure that conflicts will always reach a final and mutually acceptable solution. Even so, the fact remains that the kinds of limitations noted here in the conflict management mechanisms of IGOs would need to be seriously addressed if the international community is to have any chance of promoting, maintaining, or restoring peace within a strife-torn region. With these caveats in mind, and with the experiences of other IGOs providing a background, let us now turn to examine the conflict management machinery of the OAU and OAS.

Notes

1. The demand for UN peace-keepers is on the rise. Thirteen peace-keeping operations were established between 1945 and 1987. Another 13 were established between 1987 and the beginning of 1992. By 1999, the UN had been involved in not less than 30 operations.
2. Boutros Boutros-Ghali, *An Agenda for Peace* (New York: United Nations, 1992), pp. 35-37.
3. Robert W. Macdonald, *The League of Arab States: A Study in the Dynamics of Regional Organization* (Princeton: Princeton University Press, 1965), p. 241.

Chapter 3

OAU and OAS Machinery for Conflict Management

THIS chapter is concerned with an examination of the conflict management machinery of the OAU and OAS. It assesses the extent to which the two organisations have made adequate provision for effective action at all three stages of the conflict management circle. The overview of conflict management by some IGOs, undertaken in the last chapter, has provided some context for the analysis in this chapter.

The OAU and OAS are multi-purpose organisations committed to the pursuit of a wide range of objectives. From their respective charters, it would seem that the activities of the two organisations cover almost all aspects of human endeavour, from political, economic, educational, social, cultural, scientific, and technological issues, to the management of conflicts and the overall defence and security of their regions. Member states are expected to cooperate in all these fields and work together toward achieving regional prosperity. While both the OAU and OAS have thus been ambitious in terms of role acceptance, there is a marked disparity in the means provided by the two organisations for the realisation of their respective goals. In this regard, the OAS has certainly been more generously endowed than the OAU.

Another contrast exists between the two organisations. The OAS Charter evolved from a long history of fruitful co-operation among the countries of the Americas, and so benefited from the experiences and instruments governing the various areas of co-operation. In contrast, the framers of OAU had no documented history of continental co-operation on which to draw and were inspired chiefly by hopes – often extravagant hopes – for a bright post-colonial future.

The OAS, which is the world's oldest surviving regional IGO, evolved out of the Pan-American movement that started with the Congress of Panama in 1826 and blossomed in the first half of the

20th century. The OAS was established in 1948 at the Ninth International Conference of American States in Bogota, Colombia. Before the organisation was given its present name; it was referred to at various times as the Inter-American System, the Internal Union of American Republics, and the Pan-American Union. During this early period member states signed not less than eight instruments relating to various areas of co-operation.

- The Treaty to Avoid or Prevent Conflicts Between the American States, Signed on May 3, 1923.
- The General Convention of Inter-American Conciliation, Signed on January 5, 1929.
- The General Treaty of Inter-American Arbitration and Additional Protocol of Progressive Arbitration, signed on January 5, 1929.
- The Anti-War Treaty of Non-Aggression and Conciliation, signed on October 10, 1933.
- The Additional Protocol to the General Convention of Inter-American Conciliation, signed on December 26, 1933.
- The Convention to Co-ordinate, Extend and Assure the Fulfilment of the Existing Treaties Between the American States, signed on December 23, 1936.
- The Inter-American Treaty on Good Offices and Mediation, signed on December 23, 1936.
- The Treaty on the Prevention of Controversies, signed on December 23, 1936.

In contrast to this extensive record of regional co-operation among the long established States of the American hemisphere, countries that had only recently emerged from colonial rule formed the OAU. Admittedly, the OAU evolved from the Pan-African movement, which started in earnest during World War II. That notwithstanding, the organisation had no conventions or instruments of past co-operative ventures among its member states to look up to when it was established in 1963 at the Assembly of Africa's Heads of State and Government in Addis Ababa,

Ethiopia. Despite this difference, however, the machinery set up by the two organisations for conflict management has much in common. Apparently the OAU benefited from the experience of the OAS. As is discussed at greater length below, both organisations generally follow the same pattern of conflict management as other IGOs, such as the use of Council of Ministers and ad hoc committees of selected Heads of State. They have, however, gone a step further by creating what could be regarded as mediatory organs. Thus, at least on paper, the conflict management instruments established by the OAU and OAS entail a more comprehensive coverage of the conflict management circle.

The OAU

Although the OAU's conflict management machinery covers all stages within the conflict management circle, the level of coverage at the different stages varies. In the area of peace promotion and conflict prevention, the OAU evolved what could be regarded as a behavioural code to order the relationship between its member states and to create a climate of peace in Africa. The Charter of the Organisation of African Unity embodies the following principles:

- Recognition of the sovereign equality of all member states.
- Non-interference in the internal affairs of member states.
- Respect for the sovereignty and territorial integrity of each state and for its inalienable right of independent existence.
- Peaceful settlement of disputes by negotiation, mediation, conciliation, or arbitration.
- Unreserved condemnation, in all its forms, of political assassination as well as subversive activities on the part of a neighbouring or any other state.[1]

In subsequent years, the OAU added to these rules as it became apparent that the original principles were unable to prevent conflict between member states. One area that soon became troublesome related to the boundaries that member states had inherited from the former colonial powers. Within the first year of the establishment of the OAU, Africa witnessed no less than six boundary conflicts, three of which led to violent clashes (Morocco-Algeria, Ethiopia-Somalia, and Kenya-Somalia).

The first issue the organisation had to address, then, was the border question. At the Cairo Summit in July 1964, the OAU passed a resolution that enjoined member states to respect their inherited boundaries upon the attainment of independence. Later measures that likewise became part of OAU's behavioural code were the declaration against subversion, passed at the Accra Summit in October 1965 and the resolution on the problem of refugees passed at the Kinshasa Summit in 1967.[2]

These measures represent only some of the possible responses at the level of peace promotion and conflict prevention within the conflict management circle. There are still other measures, in the area of integrative planning and confidence-building, that could help to consolidate the OAU's behavioural code so that African states might better appreciate the organic connection between these principles and their individual national interests.

The need to promote mutual trust among African states cannot be overemphasised, given the long history of their colonially-imposed mutual isolation. Africa was for many years under the colonial tutelage of no fewer than seven West European powers, each of which carried out a different form of political socialisation in its colonies. During the long period of colonial rule, these powers also formalised and entrenched an unequal vertical economic relationship with their African colonies, in which the rural economy of the latter was tied to the industrial economy of the former. This led to the collapse of pre-colonial economic and political ties between African states. And because horizontal intra-African interactions were not encouraged, when African states became independent they found themselves strangers to one another, especially from those states that had different colonial masters.

This situation has not changed much since independence, despite the formation of the OAU. The few interactions that take place are limited to government officials, and these usually occur at summit or ministerial council meetings, diplomatic cocktail parties, or at meetings of the joint commissions and agencies of the organisation. As far as ordinary African citizens are concerned, the OAU has yet to have any meaningful impact in terms of facilitating contact with nationals of other African countries. In fact, African professionals interact more easily with extra-African, especially western, professionals than with their African counterparts. Until conditions can be created to ensure maximum contact and interaction between Africans of all grades and professions, it will be difficult for the OAU to eradicate the mutual suspicion and distrust that persist among African states. An important area in which the OAU could move toward creating the necessary conditions to permit multifaceted and constant intra-African interactions is through the development of communication infrastructures. To this end, the trans-African highway project could be resurrected, customs and immigration laws harmonised, and cross-border travel made considerably easier.

Facilitating regional integration would help to minimise the number and effects of border conflicts. African states need to be weaned away from the notion of territorial exclusiveness and encouraged to favour the "bridge" concept of international boundaries. Under the bridge concept, boundary lines are seen not as monuments of separation and division but as points of contact that permit exchange, interaction, and the joint exploitation of shared resources along international borders.[3]

It is encouraging to note that African states have recently shown increasing interest in forging regional economic integration. Between 1980, when the Lagos Plan of Action was drawn up, projecting the formation of an African common market by the year 2000, and the June 1991 OAU Summit in Abuja, Nigeria, nothing had been done to move toward this goal. At Abuja, however, African leaders demonstrated remarkable enthusiasm in signing "Africa's Economic Community Treaty." Even though it was not ratified before the OAU transited into what is now called the African Union (AU), it is to be hoped that the renewed enthusiasm that has greeted its transformation into AU would be sustained in the years ahead to facilitate Africa's drive toward full integration.

As regards the other two stages within the conflict management circle – conflict control and conflict resolution – the machinery of the OAU essentially revolves around the Commission of Mediation, Conciliation, and Arbitration (CMCA), which was established under Article XIX of the organisation's charter. Other organs whose functions touch on the conflict management activities of the OAU are the Assembly of Heads of State and Government, the Council of Ministers, the General Secretariat and the Defence Commission. A critical examination of the conflict management roles of the OAU's various organs reveals a division of labour between the CMCA, which operates within the area of conflict resolution, and the other bodies, which work within the area of conflict control and abatement.

The Assembly of Heads of State and Government

The Assembly of Heads of State and Government comprises the heads of state and government of member states or "their fully accredited representatives". It represents the supreme organ of the OAU that is charged with the responsibility to discuss and take decisions on all matters of common concern to Africa.[4] In other words, it is the final authority on all matters brought before the organisation. The specific functions of the assembly in relation to the conflict management activities of the OAU are not stated in the charter. The only reference to the Assembly in this connection is in the Protocol of the CMCA. In that protocol, it is stated that "a dispute may be referred to the Commission jointly by the parties concerned, by a party to the dispute, by the Council of Ministers, or by the Assembly of Heads of State and Government."[5]

The Assembly, it seems, is expected to refer conflicts to the CMCA for settlement. Of course, this does not mean that the assembly cannot take such measures it deems fit to abate a conflict. Those measures might be in the form of appeals to the parties involved in the conflict to exercise restraint and desist from any action that could escalate the conflict, or they might be resolutions directed toward getting parties already in conflict to halt hostilities and withdraw to their previous positions. The Assembly might also decide to establish a peacekeeping force to separate the parties. Although these functions are not spelled out, they are generally understood as the normal organisational conflict management response at the level of the Assembly.

For operational purposes, there is embodied in the OAU arrangement a provision for the "Office of the Current Chairman". Under the rules of procedure of the Assembly, there is provision for a "Bureau of the Assembly" made up of nine members, including the current chairman, who is expected to head the Bureau. Both the chairman and the other members of the Bureau are expected to serve until the next summit is convened, at which a new Bureau is elected. Between summits, the Bureau could serve as a readily available organ for the organisation's management of conflicts between its members.

The Council of Ministers

The Council of Minister comprises foreign ministers or "such other Ministers as are designated by the Governments of Member States". It is charged with the responsibility to implement the decisions of the Assembly, "take cognisance of any matter referred to it by the Assembly," and " co-ordinate inter-African co-operation in accordance with the instructions of the Assembly."[6] There are no specific statements about the role the Council of Ministers should play in relation to the conflict management activities of the OAU, except for two references in the CMCA Protocol. One of such references is that the Council may submit disputes to the CMCA for settlement. The other concerns cases in which a dispute has been referred to the CMCA and one or more of the parties refuse to submit to the jurisdiction of the commission, in which instance the CMCA "shall refer the matter to the Council for consideration."[7] In essence, therefore, the Council's role does not also go beyond taking palliative measures.

The General Secretariat

The General Secretariat is similarly not given any special conflict management role in the charter. The head of the General Secretariat is the administrative secretary-general (simply referred to as secretary-general). As the title implies, he is charged with the responsibility of directing the affairs of the secretariat.

However, Rule 9 of the "Functions and Regulations of the

Secretariat" implies some form of participation by the secretary-general in the deliberations of the organs of the OAU. According to the relevant clause, "the participation of the secretary-general in the deliberations of the Assembly, of the Council of Ministers, of the Specialised Commissions and other organs of the Organisation shall be governed by the provisions of the Charter and by the respective Rules of Procedure of these bodies." By participating in the deliberations of the relevant organs of the organisation, the secretary-general cannot but be involved in the conflict management efforts of the OAU. Obviously, as the official representative of the organisation and the reporter to the principal organs of the organisation, the office of the secretary-general has an obligation as well as the implicit responsibility to be involved in OAU's conflict management efforts. In this sense, it can take pre-emptive action to control the escalation of conflict that may erupt between meetings of the Council of Ministers and the Assembly of Heads of State and Government.

The Defence Commission

There is little elaboration on the functions of the Defence Commission in the OAU Charter, nor does the commission have a separate protocol like that of the CMCA. All that is said about the Commission in the Charter is that it is charged with the responsibility "to take cognisance of any question referred to it by the Assembly and the Council of Ministers." Also, the Commission is "to promote inter-African co-operation in defence matters, in accordance with the directives of the Assembly and Council of Ministers."[8] As an organ responsible for the military-related activities of the OAU, the commission's involvement in conflict management lies in the area of peace-keeping. As contained in the next chapter, the OAU has been miserably ineffective in developing a viable programme of collective troop mobilisation in Africa.

Commission of Mediation, Conciliation and Arbitration (CMCA)

The responsibility of effecting the resolution of conflicts in Africa was placed at the door of the CMCA. The establishment of the

CMCA is a clear demonstration of the seriousness with which African states took conflict management as a key function of OAU. Unfortunately, however, the Commission was not effectively utilised.

Established under Article XIX of the OAU Charter, the Commission was to comprise 21 members appointed by the Assembly of Heads of State and Government from among qualified nationals of member states. Each commissioner was to serve for five years and could be re-appointed. The Assembly was also to appoint a president from among the commissioners, as well as two vice-presidents, who were to form the Bureau of the Commission and serve on a full-time basis. The other members of the commission were to serve part-time. The commission was then to appoint a registrar to staff at its administrative office, located in Addis Ababa, the OAU headquarters.

The CMCA was only to have jurisdiction over disputes between states, which it could deal with through either mediation, conciliation, or arbitration. The Protocol of the CMCA established rigid procedures to be adopted under each of these approaches, thereby severely limiting the commission's flexibility.[9]

The enthusiasm that member states exhibited in setting up the CMCA at the inaugural meeting of the OAU in 1963 was not carried forward into the practical establishment of the Commission. The CMCA Protocol was not adopted until July 21, 1964, at the Cairo Summit. The appointment of the principal members took a further year, occurring during the Accra Summit of December 1965, and the process of appointing its principal officials was not fully completed until 1968, at the Algiers Summit. The inaugural meeting of the Commission was not held until December 1967. And the Council of Ministers only approved the regular budget proposed for the Commission in February 1968. As the next chapter describes, all these delays had an adverse effect on the work of the CMCA.

Although the CMCA was not, strictly speaking, constituted as a judicial organ, its membership tended to give it that outlook and complexion. According to the CMCA Protocol, "members of the Commission shall be persons with recognised professional qualifications."[10] Although no mention was made of any specific profession, it turned out that all those appointed to serve in the Commission were legal experts. The first president of the Commission, Justice M. A. Odesanya, was a judge of the Supreme Court of Nigeria. The two vice-presidents were William Cornelius Daniels, the Director of Legal Studies and a lecturer in Law at the University of Ghana, and Auguste Roch N'Gandzadi, the Attorney-General of the Congo. These appointments created the impression that the CMCA was a judicial outfit – an impression which, as will be seen later, made member- states reluctant to use its services.

In short, although the establishment of the CMCA reflected an appreciation on the part of OAU's founders of the need for what this study terms a mediation organ, the composition of the Commission and the procedures laid down for its work undermined its potential usefulness as a problem-solving body.

The OAS

The conflict management machinery of the OAS hinges on three treaties. These include:

1. the Charter of the Organisation of American States, which was signed in May 1948 and amended in 1967 and 1985;
2. the Inter-American Treaty of Reciprocal Assistance, otherwise known as the Rio Treaty, which was signed in September 1947; and
3. the American Treaty on Pacific Settlement, commonly referred to as the Pact of Bogota, signed in April 1948.

Enough countries did not, however, ratify the Pact of Bogota for it to be enforced. Under the OAS Charter, the member states pledged themselves to the peaceful settlement of disputes through "direct negotiation, good offices, mediation, investigation and conciliation, judicial settlement, arbitration, and those [procedures] which the parties to the dispute may especially agree upon at any time."[11] It is in the Pact of Bogota that the specific procedures for each means of settlement are articulated. The Rio Treaty has a dual purpose; while acting primarily as a collective defence pact, it also includes a provision for the peaceful resolution of conflicts.

Like the system established by the OAU, the OAS's conflict management machinery covers all stages of the conflict management circle (although whether it does so effectively is again, like the case of OAU, another matter). At the stage of peace promotion and conflict prevention, the OAS established various principles in the form of a "peace code" to order the behaviour of its members. These principles include:

- respect for the values, personality, sovereignty, and independence of each state;
- the inalienable right of each state to choose, without external interference, its political, economic, and social system and to organise itself in the way best suited to it;
- condemnation of joint action against aggression;
- peaceful settlement of disputes; and
- economic cooperation.[12]

The substance of these declarations is very similar to that of the OAU's behavioural code. However, unlike the OAU Charter, which insists on non-interference in the internal affairs of member-states, the OAS Charter includes provisions that actually recommend particular political arrangements as a way of promoting internal peace in its member states. The relevant provisions include:

- a declaration that the organisation of political arrangements in each state should be on the basis of the "effective exercise of representative democracy";
- the encouragement of social justice and social security, which are the basis of lasting peace; and
- a commitment to uphold the fundamental rights of the individual, without distinction as to race, nationality, creed, or sex.

Clearly, some of these principles, especially if attempts were to be made to try and enforce them, could be regarded by member-states as interference in their internal affairs. There also seems to be a conflict, or at least ambivalence, between these declarations and the OAS Charter's assertion of the right of each state to choose and organise its own political, economic, and social system.

In practice, however, problems arise not so much from any contradictions among the organisation's principles or from attempts at their enforcement, as from the tendency of member-states to ignore them. For instance, the framers of the OAS Charter were emphatic on the issue of non-interference in the internal affairs of member-states. Apart from including it as one of the general principles of the organisation under Article 3 of the Charter, there was further elaboration of the principle under Articles 18 through 20. Article 18 states:

> No State or group of States has the right to intervene, directly or indirectly, for any reason whatever, in the internal or external affairs of any other state. The foregoing principle prohibits not only armed force but also any other form of interference or attempted threat against the personality of the State or against its political, economic, and cultural elements.

Article 19 goes further:

> No State may use or encourage the use of coercive measures of an economic or political character in order to force the sovereign will of another State and obtain from it advantages of any kind.

And Article 20 asserts:

> The territory of a State is inviolable; it may not be the object, even temporarily, of military occupation or of other measures of force taken by another State, directly or indirectly, on any grounds whatever. No territorial acquisitions or special advantages obtained either by force or by other means of coercion shall be recognised.

Yet, despite these unambiguous declarations, interference in the internal affairs of member states has been, and remains, a frequent occurrence that the OAS is unable to halt. The main culprit in this regard has been the United States, from which the OAS receives a very substantial proportion of its resources. As a superpower, the United States has taken the liberty of acting unilaterally as the region's policeman, determined to impose a Pax-Americana on its smaller neighbours in disregard to the relevant clauses of the OAS Charter. Writing of the history of military intervention in the American hemisphere, Andrew Scott has observed that "the stronger nations do not adhere to the principle of non-intervention, and the weaker nations do not desire strict adherence."[13] While one may wonder whether at least some weaker nations might desire, but are unable to enforce non-interference, there is some truth in Scott's characterisation. It should also be pointed out that the United States is by no means the only member of the OAS to have violated the prohibition on interference.

Unlike the OAS, in which the asymmetry of power between the United States and the other member-states colours almost all calculations and actions, the OAU is not overshadowed by a regional hegemony. The very prospect of the emergence of any such overly powerful member-state led the founding fathers of the OAU to include in its charter a provision that no member, however wealthy, "shall be assessed an amount exceeding twenty percent of the yearly regular budget of the Organisation."[14]

Perhaps a viable way that the OAS can hope to cultivate greater respect for such principles as non-interference is to support them with a variety of integrative and confidence-building measures. Until member-states share the conviction that their interests and destinies are inextricably intertwined, it will be difficult to avoid the mutual distrust, petty jealousies, and rivalry that tend to undermine harmonious relationships in the region.

In the areas of conflict control and resolution, OAS procedures are articulated in the Rio Treaty and the Pact of Bogota. The relevant aspect of the Rio Treaty relates to those clauses that emphasise the organisation's commitment to the peaceful settlement of conflicts. Under Article 2 of the treaty, the members "undertake to submit every controversy which may arise between them to methods of peaceful settlement and to endeavour to settle any such controversy among themselves by means of the procedures in force in the inter-American System before referring it to the General Assembly or the Security Council of the United Nations." Article 7 states that in the case of a conflict between two or more American States, "the High Contracting Parties, meeting in consultation, shall call upon the contending States to suspend hostilities and restore matters to the *status quo ante bellum*, and shall take in addition all other necessary measures to re-establish or maintain inter-American peace and security and for the resolution of the conflict by peaceful means." As will be seen in chapter 6, most of the efforts by the OAS at peaceful settlement have been handled under the provisions of the Rio Treaty.

It is, however, under the provisions of the Pact of Bogota that all the procedures for the peaceful settlement of disputes are systematically articulated and itemised. The pact lays out in considerable detail the procedures to be followed in any of the following methods of settlement: good offices and mediation, investigation and conciliation, judicial settlement and arbitration. The arrangement is such that if one procedure fails to achieve the desired settlement, the parties should proceed to utilise the other methods until the conflict is resolved. The process ends with compulsory judicial settlement by the ICJ or compulsory and binding arbitration. The ICJ is normally to be the court of last resort. There is, however, a provision in the Pact that if the ICJ declines jurisdiction, then the parties should submit to a binding arbitration irrespective of whether or not the controversy is of a judicial nature.[15] The idea behind the elaborate arrangement, as succinctly put in the OAS Charter, is to ensure that "no dispute between American States may remain without definitive settlement within a reasonable period of time"[16]

It would seem that the Pact of Bogota, by providing excessive details in the steps to be followed under each mode of settlement, denies the OAS some flexibility. At the same time, there is a degree of inescapability once the parties to a conflict submit themselves to the procedures set out in the Pact. Submission to the procedures laid out in the Pact would seem to involve a partial surrender of sovereignty, which many countries are not prepared to do. Perhaps this rigidity and the detailed nature of the procedures outlined in the Pact, account for its almost total neglect in favour of the Rio

Treaty. Little wonder that one observer has referred to the Pact as "a monument of impractical perfectionism."[17]

As far as institutional provision for the management of conflict is concerned, a variety of bodies have had roles to play. These include the General Assembly; the Meeting of Consultation of Ministers of Foreign Affairs; the Permanent Council of the Organisation; the Advisory Defence Committee; the Inter-American Defence Board; the General Secretariat; and the Inter-American Peace Committee.

The General Assembly

The General Assembly is the supreme organ of the OAS. The charter is not precise about the level of representation at the assembly, but simply states that "all member States have the right to be represented in the General Assembly," and that "each State has the right to one vote."[18] The General Assembly replaces what used to be known as the Inter-American Conference in the organisation's original charter of 1948. This change came in 1967 at a special conference in Buenos Aires.

The exact role of the Assembly in relation to the peaceful settlement of conflicts by the OAS is not specified in the charter. However, among the duties of the Assembly, as outlined in the charter, are "to decide the general action and policy of the Organisation, determine the structure and functions of its organs, and consider any matter relating to friendly relations among the American States."[19] Thus, as the supreme organ of the OAS to which all the principal organs, especially the Meeting of Consultation of Ministers of Foreign Affairs and the Permanent Council report, the Assembly has the final authority on all matters, including those relating to peaceful settlement of conflicts.

The Meeting of Consultation of Ministers of Foreign Affairs

According to the charter, the Meeting of Consultation of Ministers of Foreign Affairs, "shall be held in order to consider problems of an urgent nature and of common interest to the American States, and to serve as the organ of consultation."[20] Like the Assembly, the exact role of the Meeting of Consultation is not spelled out in the charter; neither is it specified in the Pact of Bogota where the peaceful settlement procedures of the OAS are articulated. This means that its conflict management role must derive from its general responsibility to consider all problems of common interest to American states.

While the charter is silent on the role of the Meeting of Consultation in relation to pacific settlement, it is quite specific on its role in relation to collective defence. According to the relevant section, in case of an armed attack on the territory of an American state, the chairman of the Permanent Council shall without delay call a meeting of the Council. The Council will then decide on the convocation of a Meeting of Consultation to determine what action to take.[21] The role of the Meeting of Consultation is further elaborated in the Rio Treaty, which states that if the territorial integrity of an American state is violated, the Meeting of Consultation shall be summoned immediately to agree on the measures to be taken to assist the victim of aggression and to maintain the peace and security of the continent.[22] The treaty goes further to itemise the possible measures which the Organ of Consultation could take, such as the recall of chiefs of diplomatic missions, breaking of diplomatic or consular relations, partial or complete interruption of economic relations or of rail, sea, air, postal, telegraphic, telephonic, and radiotelephonic or radiotelegraphic communications, and the use of force.[23]

Interestingly, it is under the Rio Treaty that mention is made of the role of the Meeting of Consultation in relation to pacific settlement. The treaty states that in the case of a conflict between two or more American states, the Meeting of Consultation "shall call upon the contending states to suspend hostilities and restore matters to the *status quo ante bellum,* and shall take, in addition, all other necessary measures to establish or maintain Inter-American peace and security and for the solution of the conflict by peaceful means."[24]

Under the Rio Treaty, the conflict management role of the Meeting of Consultation of the Ministers of Foreign Affairs is quite flexible. The Meeting of Consultation is allowed great flexibility to apply any settlement technique or procedure to deal with any conflict arising between the members of the OAS. The fact that in such circumstances, the Meeting of Consultation can be convened by any member, or in the event of an armed attack by the chairman of the Permanent Council, is an added advantage. These provisions under the Rio Treaty contrast with the rigid procedures laid down in the Pact of Bogota. Apparently, it is this flexibility that has led to the treaty being used far more frequently than the Pact in the conflict management efforts of the OAS.

The Permanent Council of the Organisation

The Permanent Council of the Organisation represents the executive organ of the OAS. It has the primary responsibility under the organisation's charter to settle any conflict that may occur between member-states. The Council is composed of one representative of each member-state, "especially appointed by the respective Government, with the rank of ambassador."[25] Among its prescribed roles, are to keep vigilance over the maintenance of friendly relations among the member states and to assist them in the peaceful settlement of their disputes.[26] In performing its conflict management role, the Council may provide its good offices, set up ad hoc committees, and investigate the facts in the disputes brought before it.[27] And where the procedure for peaceful settlement of disputes recommended by the Council or its ad hoc committee is unacceptable to one party, or fails to settle the conflict, the Council "shall so inform the General Assembly, without prejudice to it taking steps to secure agreement between the parties or to restore relations between them."[28] From the provisions in the OAS Charter and the Pact of Bogota, it is clear that the council is given broad powers to assist in the peaceful settlement of disputes that may come before the OAS.

The Advisory Defence Committee

The OAS provides for an Advisory Defence Committee to advise the Organ of Consultation on problems of military co-operation that may arise in connection with the application of existing special treaties on collective security. The Committee, which has so far existed only on paper, is composed of the highest military authorities of the participating States in the Meeting of Consultation. The meeting of the Committee is expected to be held under the same conditions as the Organ of Consultation, when the latter deals with matters relating to defence against aggression.[29] Even though the prescribed role of the Committee is mainly in the area of defence and enforcement actions, it could be a suitable organ for the organisation of peace-keeping operations intended to aid in the pacific settlement efforts of the OAS. To date, however, given the nature of civil-military politics in many Latin American countries,[30] and the desire by most OAS members to mitigate the dominance of the United States in most of the Inter-American defence mechanisms, most member-states tend to favour the UN mechanisms for peace-keeping operations.

The Inter-American Defence Board

The Inter-American Defence Board (IADB) predates the OAS, having been established in 1942 to study and recommend measures for the defence of the hemisphere during World War II. Its present role, at least on paper, is principally to plan for the collective defence of the hemisphere and to contribute to strengthening the bonds of military co-operation and solidarity among the nations of the Americas.[31] As a response to wartime needs, the IADB was not originally intended to become a permanent body. However, the outbreak of the cold war in the aftermath of World War II led to the decision in 1948 to formally establish the Board as a permanent institution of the OAS.[32] Even though that decision was taken at the inaugural meeting that drew up the instruments of the OAS, no mention was made of the IADB in the OAS Charter.

The IADB is composed of a Council of Delegates drawn from twenty member-states. With headquarters in Washington, D.C., the Boards' chairman is always a general officer chosen from "the Armed Forces of the American State in which the Board has its seat"[33] – in other words, the United States always appoints the chairman. The IADB has a separate secretariat with its own staff, and it runs the Inter-American Defence College.

Among the issues that have been considered by the Council of Delegates are programmes of joint training and joint military planning, the situation in the Malvinas/Falkland Islands, terrorism and terrorist threats in the hemisphere, the drug problem, and the clandestine arms trade in the region. Because of the Board's main concern with hemispheric defence planning and with running the Inter-American Defence College, the IADB is widely perceived to have no functional role within the OAS mechanism for conflict management. However, given its set up, that is, its composition and security-related responsibilities, the IADB seems the most appropriate body to service the peace-keeping activities of the OAS. In this regard, proper co-ordination of the activities of the IADB and the Defence Advisory Committee becomes absolutely necessary. In fact, with the end of the cold war and the demise of the Soviet threat, it is possible that the IADB will increasingly take on contingency planning for possible peace-keeping missions. Since the end of the cold war relieves the IADB of its anti-communist focus, the Board is obviously placed in a better position to play a more active role in the conflict management activities, and hence peace-keeping functions, of the OAS. Already, by 1991, the Board's staff had prepared "Manuals on the IADB's Organisation and Procedures for Peace-keeping Missions, and the Conduct of Representatives of the IADB who are not Associated with Peace-keeping Operations" for presentation to the Council of Delegates.[34] Prior to the preparation of the manuals, the IADB and the United Nations International Peace Academy had organised two seminars, one in March 1979 and the other in May 1981, on "Peace-keeping and the Changing Dynamics of Security", at which the potential future role of the Board was articulated.[35] Whether the Board will, indeed, develop its role as a valuable resource for OAS peace-keeping operations will depend on the extent to which member-states are prepared to take advantage of the increasing improvement of the international political climate to redirect the focus of the IADB from a purely defence-related role to conflict management-related activities.

The General Secretariat

The General Secretariat is responsible for servicing the activities of all the principal organs of the OAS. It also serves as the custodian of the organisation's documents and archives, as well as a depository of its treaties and agreements. The secretariat is headed by a Secretary-General who is elected by the General Assembly for a five-year term and "may not be re-elected more than once or succeeded by a person of the same nationality". There is provision in the charter for the Secretary-General to "participate with voice but without vote in all meetings of the Organisation."[36]

The General Secretariat is not given any specific role in the organisation's conflict management efforts, except that the Secretary-General "may bring to the attention of the General Assembly or the Permanent Council, any matter which in his opinion might threaten the peace and security of the hemisphere or the development of the member-states."[37] As with the General Secretariat of the OAU, this means that it is through its function of reporting to, alerting, and participating (in the person of the Secretary-General) in the meetings of the General Assembly and the Permanent Council that the General Secretariat becomes effectively involved in conflict management activities. Its responsibility for implementing the decisions of the OAS also effectively involves the secretariat in conflict management activities. In recent times, especially from the late 80s, the OAS Secretary-General, Joao Clemente Baena Soares, has taken a strong personal leadership role in mediating conflicts (for instance, in Nicaragua) and promoting peace (for example, through electoral observation in Nicaragua, Paraguay, and Suriname).

The Inter-American Peace Committee

The Inter-American Peace Committee (IAPC) (known until July 1949 as the Inter-American Committee on Methods for the Peaceful Solution of Conflicts) represented a unique organ within the OAS system. It was not featured in any of the instruments of the organisation. Indeed, according to some scholars, it was established with little concept of the important role it was to play in the conflict management efforts of the OAS.[38] The instrument setting up the IAPC was passed at the Second Meeting of Ministers of Foreign Affairs in Havana in July 1940. Resolution XIV, which was introduced by the Haitian delegation, urged the Governing Board of the Pan-American Union (the predecessor of the Council of the OAS) to set up a committee composed of representatives of five countries. The committee is to be charged with the responsibility of "keeping constant vigilance to ensure that states between which any dispute exists or may arise, of any nature whatsoever, may solve it as quickly as possible, and of suggesting the measures and steps which may be conducive to a settlement." The instrument setting up the IAPC did not establish any formal procedures for its operations beyond requiring it to report its activities to the periodic International Conferences of American States and the Meetings of Foreign Ministers; from its beginnings, then, the committee enjoyed some degree of flexibility in its operations.

After constituting the membership of the committee to include Argentina, Brazil, Cuba, Mexico, and the United States, and establishing its seat in Washington, D.C., the Governing Board took no further action to activate the committee until September 1947. At that time, in response to a proposition by the Ambassador of the Dominican Republic, the five states appointed to serve in the committee named their representatives. The following year, Luis Quintanilla of Mexico was appointed the committee's chairman.

Not until 1954, at the 10th Inter-American Conference in Caracas was the Permanent Council asked to prepare a formal statute to govern the activities of the IAPC. The request was made in recognition of the growing importance of the committee, which had successfully managed a number of conflicts brought before the OAS. The new statute, which was approved in 1956, provided for the regular rotation of the membership of the committee, with one new member being elected each year for a term of five years.[39] The new statute imposed many restrictions on the IAPC which adversely affected its effective performance.[40] Previously, the committee could take up a case without needing the formality of approval by the council of the OAS; all that was required was a request from a single state, which did not even have to be a party to the dispute. Untrammelled by procedural regulations dictating a particular approach, the committee could investigate to ascertain the facts of the conflict, or it could provide good offices to bring the parties in conflict to the negotiating table, or it could attempt conciliation or mediation. Under the new statute, only a party directly involved in a conflict could request the intervention of the IAPC, and the committee could intervene only if the other party or parties to the conflict consented. These changes in the status of the IAPC (including its change of name to the "Inter-American Committee on Peaceful Settlement" (IACPS), were incorporated into the 1967 revision of the OAS Charter.[41] The effect of these changes was to obstruct and undermine the effectiveness of the IAPC as a mediatory or conciliatory organ, and member-states showed themselves no longer willing to bring their conflicts to the committee.[42] As a consequence, when the charter was further revised in 1985, the IACPS disappeared from the charter, its role being given to ad hoc committees.

Conclusion

The OAS and OAU have both made institutional provisions for the management of conflict at all stages of the conflict management circle. At the level of conflict prevention, they, like a number of other IGOs, have sought to encourage a peaceful atmosphere and overcome mistrust within their respective regions. However, their efforts to develop practical integrative activities that could build confidence and trust have often proved half-hearted and haphazard. Thus, the visionary goals of 19th century pan-Americans, like Simon Bolivar, and 20th century pan-Africans, like Kwame Nkrumah, are both still far from realisation in a climate of provincialism and narrow self-interest.

As for meeting the needs of conflict control, it should be noted that some of the institutions established by the OAU and OAS are not tailored strictly toward conflict management but rather are meant to respond to the defence needs of the two organisations. Neither organisation has yet to fully recognise the possibilities of using bodies such as the OAS's IADB and Advisory Defence Committee and the OAU's Defence Commission in such vital areas of conflict management as peace-keeping.

Unlike almost all other IGOs (the CSCE is an exception), the OAS and OAU have demonstrated an awareness of the need for a mediatory or conciliatory organ in their conflict management systems, setting up the IAPC and the CMCA, respectively. Unfortunately, as succeeding chapters show, both organisations undermined their good intentions by the kinds of structures and methods they imposed on their mediatory organs. The CMCA was constituted as a judicial outfit and not as an organ capable of exploring the problem-solving techniques of conflict management. The IAPC was derailed when member states, responding to the relative success of the IAPC's earlier effort, imposed a rigid statute on it which had the unintended effect of crippling the organ.

In the following two chapters, we will see how the conflict management machinery of both organizations fared in practice.

Notes

1. Article III of the *Charter of the Organisation of African Unity* (hereafter OAU Charter), Addis Ababa, May 25, 1963, Reprinted 1973.
2. T.A. Imobighe, *The OAU, African Defence and Security* (Benin and Owerri: Adena Publishers 1989), pp. 30-36.
3. T.A. Imobighe, "Theories and Functions of Boundaries," in B. M. Barkindo (ed.) *Management of Nigeria's Internal Boundary Questions* (Lagos: NBC Publication, 1993), pp.13-25.
4. *OAU Charter,* Articles VIII and IX.
5. *Protocol of the Commission of Mediation, Conciliation and Arbitration* (hereafter CMCA Protocol), Addis Ababa, May 1963, Reprinted 1973, Article XII.
6. *OAU Charter*, Article XIII.
7. *CMCA Protocol,* Article XII.
8. T. A. Imobighe, (1989), *op. cit.*, p. 8.
9. *CMCA Protocol,* Articles XX-XXI for mediation; Articles XXII-XXVI for conciliation; and Articles XXVII-XXXI for arbitration.
10. *Ibid.*, Article II, paragraph 3.
11. *Charter of the Organisation of American States,* as amended by the Protocols of 1967 and 1985 (hereafter OAS Charter), Article 24.

12. *Ibid.*, Article 3.
13. Andrew W. Scott, "Non-intervention and Conditional Intervention," (ed) *Journal of International Affairs* 22, No. 2 (1968), pp. 208-210.
14. *OAU Charter*, Article XXIII.
15. *The American Treaty on Pacific Settlement* (the Pact of Bogota), signed April 30, 1948, Chapters Four and Five.
16. *OAS Charter*, Article 26.
17. William L. Krieg, "Peaceful Settlement of Disputes through the Organisation of American States" (paper prepared under U.S. State Department Contract #1722-220010, Washington, D.C., Around 1974-75, no date) OAAAS Charter, Article 55.
18. *OAS Charter*, Article 55.
19. *Ibid.*, Article 53.
20. *Ibid.*, Article 60.
21. *Ibid.*, Article 64.
22. *Inter-American Treaty of Reciprocal Assistance* (the Rio Treaty), Article 6.
23. *Ibid.*, Article 8.
24. *Ibid.*, Article 7.
25. *OAS Charter*, Article 79.
26. *Ibid.*, Article 83.
27. *Ibid.*, Articles 84-86.
28. *Ibid.*, Article 87.
29. *Ibid.*, Articles 65-67.
30. The long years of military dominance of the politics of Latin American countries has led to a conscious effort on the part of the new democratic regimes in Latin America to inhibit the military, as much as possible from any pre-eminent role in OAS affairs.

31. OAS, *Annual Report of the Secretary-General, 7/1/86-6/30/87*, OEA Ser. O. III-37 Eng., (Washington D.C., General Secretariat 1986-87).
32. The permanency of the IADB was established by a resolution of the 9th International Conference of American States held in Bogota, Columbia, March 30-May 2, 1948.
33. IADB Document C-2034 Rev. I. *Regulations of the Inter-American Defence Board*, Washington, D.C. April 9, 1984, Article 5(a).
34. OAS, *Annual Report of the Secretary-General, 1990-1991*, OEA Ser. O III-41. 1990-1991 Eng. (Washington, D.C. General Secretariat, 1990-1991).
35. OAS, *Annual Report of the Secretary-General, 1979*, OEA Ser. O III-30, 1979 Eng. (Washington, D.C. General Secretariat, 1979) and Ibid., 1981-1982, OEA, OEA Ser. O III-32, 1981-1982 Eng.
36. *OAS Charter*, Articles 113 and 115 .
37. *Ibid*, Article 115.
38. Ronald L. Stechman, *The Inter-American Dilemma* (New York: Praeger, 1988), p. 67.
39. David W. Wainhouse, *International Peace Observation* (Baltimore: Johns Hopkins Press, 1966), p. 88.
40. Carlos O. Stoetzer, *The Organisation of American States: An Introduction* (New York: Praeger, 1966), pp. 34-35.
41. *OAS Revised Charter* (as amended by the Protocol of Buenos Aires, 1967), Articles 83-90.
42. Stechman, *op. cit.*, p. 68.

Chapter 4

Conflict Management by the OAU and OAS: Note on the Selection of Case Studies

AS the previous chapter detailed, the OAU and OAS have made some provisions for acting at all stages within the conflict management circle. However, as that chapter also indicated, and as the next two chapters will make abundantly clear, the effectiveness of both organisations has not been consistent across those stages. The in-depth assessments of the activities of the OAU (in chapter 5) and the OAS (in chapter 6) in a variety of cases are intended not only to document the actual methods each has employed in different situations, but also to reveal where the strengths and weaknesses of each organisation lie.

Five cases are examined for each of the organisations. All the selections were cases that had taken place by the late 1990s during which this research was concluded. The selection of these cases has been made on three bases. Firstly, their inclusion is intended to demonstrate the variety of conflict management methods employed by the OAS and OAU. Secondly, they have been chosen to illustrate both success and failure, thereby allowing some conclusions to be drawn about which circumstances and which methods seem to permit effective management by these regional bodies. And thirdly, they have been selected to represent at least part of the spectrum of conflict types to which the two regions seem susceptible.

Despite their obvious differences in terms of geography, history, geo-politics, and so forth, Africa and the Americas tend to be prone to certain types of conflict.[1] This is not to say that the frequency and intensity of those different types experienced by the two regions are the same. However, the fact remains that for various reasons – some common historical experiences and shared problems of underdevelopment being foremost among them –

the OAU and OAS face similar problems in their conflict management efforts as far as conflict types are concerned. Two studies, one of Latin America by Michael Morris and Victor Millan, the other of Africa by this author, have arrived at similar classifications of conflict.[2] According to these studies, five types[3] of conflicts can be identified:

System/Ideological Conflicts: In most cases, system conflicts erupt because of ideological differences between or among the political elite. The ensuing power struggles usually involve external forces acting in sympathy with one of the parties to the struggle. In the Americas, system conflicts were particularly common during the cold war, when the superpowers competed to spread their influence and ideological position throughout the region. The provision in the OAS Charter that each member state's political organisation should be on the basis of representative democracy and respect for human rights has given the United States a pretext for interfering in a number of regional system conflicts (ironically, however, it has not prevented the United States from fraternising with dictatorial, anti-democratic regimes, such as the Noriega's in Panama). Although system/ideological conflicts are not uncommon in Africa, they have usually not provoked frequent and violent inter-state conflicts in the continent. Part of the reason for this can be found in the adherence by OAU member states to the principle of non-interference in the internal affairs of member-states. Thus, cautious sympathy rather than open support for one or the other side in domestic struggles has often, though certainly not always, been the rule. Part of the reason also lies in the fact that Africa possesses no powerful regional hegemon.

Boundary/Territorial Conflicts: These conflicts are now more common and acute in Africa than in the American hemisphere. In the latter region, the question of borders provoked many conflicts in the 19th and early 20th centuries; but these now appear to have been more or less settled. In Africa, however, where the imperial powers withdrew only after World War II, the states are still wrestling with their inheritance of arbitrary and ill-defined boundaries from the former colonial rulers. Indeed, boundary/territorial conflicts are the most common of all types of African inter-state conflicts.

Resource Conflicts: It is often difficult to make a clear distinction between resource conflicts and boundary/territorial conflicts, the latter often being made all the more explosive by the presence of valuable resources in disputed areas. In the Americas, as Morris and Millan note, most resource conflicts relate to "tensions over energy resources and 200-mile offshore control."[4] In Africa, the asymmetrical distribution of resources has often generated jealousies and suspicions among states that have inspired inter-state disharmony.

Hegemonic/Influence Conflicts: There is a pronounced difference in the extent of hegemonic/influence conflicts within the two regions. The reason is straightforward. Africa has no hegemonic power akin to the United States with the zeal and resources to attempt to impose a particular ideology on weaker states. Among the pretenders to this role, Libya has made forceful attempts to spread its power (especially in the case of Chad), but has met with only limited success. South Africa is perhaps the nearest equivalent to a U.S–style hegemony, with a long (but now presumably past) record of involvement in struggles within the former "frontline" states. It may be noted, however, that South Africa was motivated as much, if not more by self-protection, as by a desire to impose its will on the region.

The phenomenon of external dependency (by which many African states enjoy only a semblance of independence while remaining under the economic domination of external powers) has resulted in a number of African states becoming instruments of extra-regional attempts to destabilise other African states. Within the Americas, the United States has clearly demonstrated that it has the resources and will to act as a hegemonist, intervening in the internal affairs and disputes of many Latin American countries either directly or through support of various regimes and groups. U.S hegemony reached its peak during the cold war. Now that the war has ended and most regimes in the region are on relatively friendly terms with Washington, the forceful assertion of U.S. hegemony has declined somewhat. The 1994 United States intervention in Haiti to restore President Aristide to power which was carefully orchestrated through the instrumentality of the OAS and UN is an indication that the US has greatly mellowed down its forceful arbitrary assertion of its hegemony in the hemisphere.

Migration/Refugee Conflicts: The mere fact of the migration of people across national borders does not provoke conflict. Other factors must also come into play for conflict to occur. These include the motive behind their flight namely, whether the refugees intend to carry out hostile acts against their home governments from their place of refuge, whether the host country welcomes and sympathises with the refugees; and the existing state of the relationship between the countries involved. In the American hemisphere, most inter-state conflicts arising from the problem of refugees have been spill-overs from internal conflicts. They usually occur in cases where refugees move to neighbouring countries ideologically opposed to their home government in order to build a base from which to continue their struggle against that government. In Africa, refugee problems gained prominence in the 1960s and 1970s, when more African states attained their independence from the colonial powers; and hence harbouring refugees fleeing oppressive rule was no longer likely to demonstrate anti-colonial feelings but was rather an unfriendly act toward fellow African regimes.

As the following case studies will show, very few conflicts ever fit neatly into one or the other of these five classifications. Almost invariably, conflicts are hybrids, having multiple causes (see Appendix I). What, then is the point of trying to distinguish the types of conflict that affect Africa and the Americas? There are two reasons. One is to set the stage for the case studies, by indicating the kinds of problems that confront the two regions; and the similarities between their experiences; thereby demonstrating that the case studies are not atypical. The second reason is to emphasise the complex nature of the conflicts with which the OAU and OAS have to deal, which complexity prevents their easy resolution. As such, it underscores the argument of this study that deeply rooted and multi-faceted conflicts are rarely amenable to lasting settlement through such measures as the passing of palliative resolutions, the introduction of peace-keeping forces, or adjudication by some international tribunal or court. The path to their resolution may certainly involve one or more of those measures, but it will not lead to success unless it also involves a lot of hard bargaining and interest harmonisation, in other words, problem solving.

Before moving on to examine the 10 case studies, a final word of explanation or, if the reader prefers, caution is required. The selection of cases is intended to be representative and illustrative of the kinds of conflict that bedevil the two regions and the kinds of responses they have drawn from their respective regional organisations. But it is not intended to be comprehensive. No doubt, readers will deprecate the omission of this or that case, and they may have good reasons for doing so. However, in the post-World War II period, literally dozens of inter-state conflicts have erupted in each of the two regions.[5] Providing an in-depth analysis of even a significant proportion of these conflicts is far beyond the scope and resources of this study. Within these inevitable limitations, the author has tried to choose cases that, as indicated at the outset of this chapter, together offer a fair impression of typical conflict types and typical conflict management response, whether successful and unsuccessful.

Notes

1. Conflicts, of course, can be classified in a number of ways. They can, for instance, be classified according to the level of escalation (like violent and non-violent conflicts); on the basis of the number of parties involved (like bilateral and multilateral conflicts); or on the basis of their territorial spread (like local, regional and global conflicts). Here, they are classified according to the fundamental issues involved.
2. Michael A. Morris and Victor Millan, eds., *Controlling Latin*

American Conflicts: Ten Approaches (Boulder: Westview Press, 1983), chapter 1; and T.A. Imobighe, *The OAU: African Defence and Security* (Benin and Owerri: Adena, 1989), chapter 2.

3. Some readers may question why ethnic or religious conflicts have not been included as a separate sixth classification, especially in the light of the character of many African conflicts. The important point to emphasise is that due to the nature of social stratification and the low level of integration, in Africa particularly, there is a tendency for the parties in conflict to be divided along religious or ethnic lines. This, however, does not contradict the fact that these conflicts are essentially related to disagreements over the mode of governance and resource or power sharing.

4. Morris and Millan *op. cit.*, p. 4.

5. Appendix 1 for a list of some of these conflicts.

Chapter 5

The Practice of Conflict Management by the OAU

ALTHOUGH on paper the OAU's conflict management procedures centre on the CMCA, in practice other organs of the OAU have been used in that role. Indeed, throughout the life of the commission, no member-state solicited the commission's services. Two reasons can be found to account for this mismatch between the theoretical and the pragmatic. The first has to do with the delay in making the CMCA operational, a delay which provided the OAU the opportunity to experiment with other mechanisms for the management of conflicts. Between 1963 and 1968, when the CMCA was fully operational, a number of conflicts erupted that demanded the OAU's attention. These included the conflicts between Morocco and Algeria, Somalia and Kenya, Ethiopia and Somalia, Ghana and Upper Volta (Burkina Faso), Dahomey (Benin) and Niger, Guinea and the Ivory Coast, and Rwanda and Burundi. In the absence of an operational CMCA, the OAU had to resort to a variety of ad hoc arrangements involving the Assembly of Heads of State and Government, the Council of Ministers, the Secretary-General, and temporary commissions. It would appear that, by the time the CMCA was finally ready to begin its work, OAU member-states were accustomed to ad hoc arrangements and decided to continue with them.

A second reason why the commission was never used by those same states that had agreed to its creation at the OAU's inaugural meeting is that the CMCA was perceived to be a judicial body. As noted in the previous chapter, nation-states are usually reluctant to submit themselves to the judicial processes of conflict management because to do so compromises their freedom to manoeuvre. Entirely made up of legal experts and structured as a judicial entity, the CMCA could not but be expected to favour legalistic prescriptions in its handling of conflicts. Trying to explain the reluctance of OAU member states to bring their disputes to the commission, its first president, Odesanya, observed:

> In one inter-state dispute after another, secret offers of assistance by the Commission could not induce the States involved in the disputes to submit to the jurisdiction of a body they persistently regard as judicial... I did not find it helpful the conditions of secrecy under which the Commission promises to operate nor the assurance which I have often been given that mediation and conciliation procedures do not involve the determination of right and wrong, innocence or guilt.[1]

With the CMCA always sidelined, the OAU has throughout its existence been obliged to manage conflicts through organs that were not specifically equipped for the purpose. As the following five case studies illustrate, those organs had at best only limited success.

The Algeria-Morocco Conflict (1963-1973)

Background

The conflict between Algeria and Morocco was the direct result of Morocco's irredentism. Conscious of the size of the pre-colonial Moroccan empire, which stretched from the Mediterranean coast to the Senegal River in West Africa, Morocco's leaders were anxious to enlarge the relatively small area that their post-colonial state occupied. This irredentist ambition was reinforced by a desire to have access to the rich mineral resources of some of Morocco's neighbours. In the early years of independence, the Moroccan ruling elite therefore laid claim to what they regarded as their country's "historic frontiers", which included the whole of the Spanish Sahara and Mauritania, part of Mali, as well as some parts of Algerian territory.

Three factors complicated the boundary dispute between Morocco and Algeria. One relates to the inconsistent and haphazard manner in which the French colonial administrators tried to define the border, especially after the Franco-Moroccan Treaty of 1912, under which Morocco became a French protectorate. For instance, the town of Tindouf, which formed part of the area under dispute, was formerly put within Algeria. While it was in Algeria, it remained under Franco-Moroccan administration until 1952. The French apparently believed that most of the region towards the southern border between the two countries was not habitable, and as such its delimitation was unnecessary.[2]

The second factor, which inflamed the situation, was the discovery of oil and other mineral resources on the Algerian side of the border region. In particular, a large deposit of iron ore was discovered in the Tindouf area. While all of these mineral deposits were being discovered on the Algerian side, Moroccan concessions to foreign oil companies for oil exploration did not yield any findings.[3]

The third factor that helped to complicate the border problems relates to the ideological differences between the regimes of Morocco and Algeria. Whereas Morocco retained a monarchical government and adopted a policy of economic liberalism, there emerged in Algeria a revolutionary socialist regime committed to removing all shackles of feudalism from the country In fact, between 1956 and 1962, Morocco had refrained from negotiating with France on the border issue, asserting that the delimitation of the border should await Algerian independence. After their bitter struggle for independence against French rule, the new leaders of Algeria became radicalised and did not have the slightest desire to emulate Moroccan policies. Thus, while most of the lands acquired by colonial settlers in Morocco were still owned by foreigners, the new leaders in Algeria nationalised all foreign-owned lands. The radical policies of the new regime in Algeria endeared it to the left-wing opposition in Morocco.

When hostilities broke out between the two countries in September 1963, their disagreement thus concerned not just the placement of the international boundary line, but also economic and political issues. Any lasting settlement of the conflict had, therefore, to resolve all of these issues. In particular, such a settlement had to include measures to restore mutual confidence and trust between countries whose affairs were managed by regimes with strong ideological differences.

The OAU's Response

The first initiative of the OAU came through the organisation's serving chairman, Emperor Haile Selassie. After some Moroccan hesitation in accepting the OAU's mediation, Selassie succeeded, with the co-operation of President Modibo Keita of Mali, in arranging a meeting in Bamako, the capital of Mali, on October 29-30, 1963, at which a cease-fire agreement was concluded. The main points of the Bamako Communiqué included the following:

- An immediate end to hostilities on November 2.
- The establishment of a committee (hereafter referred to as Bamako Cease-fire Committee) composed of Algerian, Moroccan, Ethiopian, and Malian Military officers, which would define a demilitarised zone.
- The supervision of security and military neutrality in the demilitarised zone by Ethiopian and Malian observers.
- A request for an extraordinary meeting of the OAU Council of Ministers for the purpose of creating a committee of arbitration to effect a definite solution to the Algeria-Morocco border dispute.
- The cessation of hostile propaganda attacks beginning from November 1.[4]

The Bamako Agreement did not immediately put an end to the hostilities. Skirmishes continued, which made the creation of a demilitarised zone problematic. After about a fortnight of consultation and persuasion, the proposed extraordinary meeting of the OAU Council of Ministers was at last convened in Addis Ababa on November 15-18, 1963. At the end of the meeting, the council passed a resolution in which it noted the fact that the CMCA was yet to be established; reaffirmed the imperative necessity for African states to settle differences by peaceful means, within a strictly African framework, and in accordance with the principles of the OAU Charter; and approved the creation of a seven-member "Special Committee" under the chairmanship of Mali to settle the conflict. The seven-member committee included

Ethiopia, Ivory Coast, Mali, Nigeria, Senegal, Sudan and Tanganyika (later Tanzania).

Even though the Bamako Agreement proposed a committee of arbitration, the Special Committee set up by the Council of Ministers did not function exactly like an arbitration panel. Because it was given the freedom to establish its own procedural rules, the committee decided it would first determine the responsibility for the outbreak of hostilities and then examine the basic causes of the conflict and submit concrete proposals to the parties for its definite settlement.[5] The Special Committee held a number of meetings with the two parties: on December 2-5, 1963, at Abidjan; on January 23-28, 1964, at Bamako; on February 22-29, 1964, at Lagos; on April 24 – May 7, 1964, at Bamako; and on October 30, 1964, in Algeria and Rabat. The last two meetings were essentially to monitor progress in the bilateral negotiations that started in May between the two parties.

On February 20, 1964, the Bamako Cease-fire Committee, which continued its efforts at creating a demilitarised zone, succeeded in procuring an agreement between the two parties that led to the withdrawal of troops to their positions prior to the outbreak of hostilities and the promise of resumption of diplomatic relations. By mid-April 1964, relations between the two countries had improved to the extent that there was an exchange of prisoners. On May 11, the two countries signed a communiqué in which they expressed satisfaction with the work of the Special committee and established a Mixed Committee at an ambassadorial level, which was to meet later that month to continue with bilateral negotiations. The two parties met from May 25 to 29 and reached agreement on the following points:

- Resumption of free passage of persons and property between the two countries.
- Return of nationals from the two countries expelled during the period of hostilities.
- Compensation of the victims of the border skirmishes.
- Return of the property of victims.
- Assistance to victims to enable them resume their normal activities.

- Lifting of all restrictions placed by the governments of either country on the liberty of the nationals of the other country.[6]

Although this agreement marked a step forward towards the normalisation of relations, the two countries were yet to resolve their border dispute. It was to take many more years of bilateral negotiations before the two countries arrived at a final settlement, on June 15, 1972, at the OAU Summit in Rabat, Morocco. Since the announcement of the final settlement, there has been relative peace along the border between the two countries. The tension that persists between the two countries is essentially due to Algerian support for the self-determination of the people of Western Sahara, a territory which has become the latest victim of Morocco's irredentist policy (more on this later in this chapter).

The Special Committee essentially acted as a facilitator, helping the parties in conflict to start and sustain the process of serious negotiations to resolve the fundamental issues involved in the conflict. After a number of meetings with the two parties, the Special Committee left the negotiations to the representatives of the two countries to work out a mutually acceptable agreement. In the end, the two countries settled the conflict through a functional arrangement that respected Algeria's right to the portions of territory in dispute, and at the same time allowed for the joint exploitation of all the mineral resources in the area within the context of Maghreb sub-regional unity. At this time, efforts to create an economic union in North Africa, to be known as the Maghreb Union, were on high gear.

Two points should be made about the way this conflict was managed. First, the final resolution of the conflict did not come suddenly. It took a decade of negotiation before the leaders of the two countries concluded a final agreement. The ability to sustain the process of negotiations over a long period to resolve all the fundamental issues involved was, therefore, crucial to effecting a lasting settlement of this conflict.

Moreover, the OAU played a minimal role in sustaining the process of negotiations over this long period, for the two countries saw the need to continue with the negotiations until they reached a mutually acceptable solution. In many cases, it should be noted, the parties to a conflict are not able to sustain this momentum on their own and require continuous external encouragement to remain at the negotiating table. Thus, an international organisation involved in conflict management needs an effective organ to help parties in conflict to sustain this momentum. Even so, the OAU played a critical role at the initial stages of the negotiations. The fact that the OAU's efforts did not stop at organising a cease-fire and creating a demilitarised zone, but went further to launch the parties on the path of serious negotiations, was vital to the successful management of the conflict.

A second point to note is that the method, which was used, in the final resolution of this conflict seems to conform to the problem-solving approach, which seeks to harmonise all the interests involved in a conflict. In this case, it was apparent that behind Morocco's irredentist policy was a strong desire to benefit from the mineral resources in the area. The recognition of this interest was critical to the solution of the problem. The process was also aided by the interest shown by the countries of the sub-region in economic integration. As was remarked earlier, the idea of creating a Maghreb Union was gaining momentum at the time.

The Rwanda-Burundi Conflict (1963-1978)

Background

The roots of the conflict between Rwanda and Burundi are many and tangled, involving ethnic tensions, movements of refugees, and ideological differences. Ultimately, perhaps, the problem between the two states can be traced to the circumstances of their territorial existence: the two countries ranking among the tiniest states in Africa, and their viability depending on their ability to work out some integrated planning with their larger, more self-sufficient neighbours.

Rwanda and Burundi are inhabited mainly by two ethnic groups – the Hutu, who form the majority of the population in the two territories, and the Tutsi. Before their colonisation, the two countries were under monarchical governments dominated by the Tutsi minority, who enjoyed a clear socio-economic ascendancy over the Hutus. During colonisation, the two territories came under German rule and formed part of the German East African Empire. When Germany was stripped of all its colonies in Africa after World War I, the two territories came under the Belgian rule, which continued even after World War II when they became United Nations Trust Territories. Throughout the period of colonial rule, the monarchical system in both countries remained intact.

In 1959, as decolonisation was proceeding, the Hutu in Rwanda carried out a violent revolt against their traditional Tutsi overlords and established a Hutu-dominated republican government. The violence that accompanied the revolt led to a large wave of migration of Tutsi across the border into Burundi. That same year, Burundi became independent under a constitutional monarchy with the Tutsi aristocracy still very much in control.

The contrasting political developments in the two countries, combined with the flood of Tutsi refugees into Burundi created an uneasy atmosphere of tension ready to explode at the slightest provocation. The situation deteriorated in late 1963 as armed Tutsi began to mass along the border between the two countries. In November and December, the Tutsi forces invaded Rwanda, seeking to overthrow its government. The Rwandan government accused Burundi of aiding and abetting the attempted invasion. The incident led to further violence against the Tutsi population in Rwanda and the aggravation of the refugee problem. Some Tutsi sought refuge in Uganda; at the height of the conflict, it was estimated that there were about 54,000 Rwandan refugees in Uganda.[7]

The OAU's Response

The conflict was brought to the attention of the OAU in February 1964 by the Ugandan government. The initial concern of the OAU was to deal with the refugee problem and reduce its potential to inspire inter-state conflict. Thus, following an appeal by the OAU Secretary-General to the two countries to settle their differences amicably, the Council of Ministers established a 10-member Commission to examine the refugee problem in Africa and make recommendations to the council on how it could be solved. The Commission was made up of Burundi, Cameroon, Democratic Republic of Congo (former Zaire) Ghana, Nigeria, Rwanda, Senegal, Sudan, Tanzania and Uganda.

No immediate attempt was made to get the two sides together to iron out their differences. Apparently, the OAU believed that the solution of the refugee problem would automatically bring about a resolution of the conflict between Rwanda and Burundi. A considerable length of time, however, was required to deal with the refugee problem through the establishment of principles to guide the acceptance of refugees by OAU member-states and regulate the activities of refugees.

The commission produced a draft convention on African refugees, which included the following principles:

- The term "refugee" should be reserved for nationals of countries whose political, racial, or religious regimes have made it necessary for them to expatriate themselves for fear of oppression, imprisonment, or any other hardship.
- Countries of asylum should not permit refugees to attack their countries of origin either through the press or the radio, or with arms. Likewise, the countries of origin should not consider the granting of asylum to refugees as an unfriendly act and should refrain from attacking the country of asylum through the press and radio, or with arms.
- Refugees should be settled as far away as possible from the frontiers adjoining their countries of origin.
- Countries that have refugee problems and whose boundaries are not clearly demarcated should take immediate steps to have such boundaries demarcated.
- Refugees who wish to return to their countries of origin should be helped to do so.
- Countries that have refugee problems should forthwith start or continue bilateral talks in order to solve them in accordance with the spirit and letter of the OAU Charter.[8]

The draft convention was presented to the fourth session of

the Council of Ministers in Nairobi, between February and March 1965, and was commended to member states for comments. At the Accra Summit in October 1965, a panel of legal experts was mandated to review the draft before its adoption at the Council of Ministers meeting in Addis Ababa in February 1969. It was then submitted for signature at the Addis Ababa Summit on September 10, 1969, as the "OAU Convention Governing the Specific Aspects of Refugee Problems in Africa" (hereafter, referred to as OAU Convention on Refugees).[9] The convention came into force on November 27, 1973, after its ratification by the required 14 states.

By setting up the commission and appealing to the two sides to exercise restraint, the OAU merely succeeded in abating the conflict for a while. In 1966, the conflict erupted again. There were reports of an impending Tutsi attack on Rwanda. Evidently, the two countries needed to enter into serious negotiations to try and resolve their differences. Thus, at the Assembly of Heads of State and Government held in the Ethiopian capital in October and November 1966, President Mobutu was requested to extend his good offices to the two parties.[10] In March 1967, Mobutu succeeded in bringing the leaders of the two countries together. They met at the border town of Gona and agreed to disarm the refugees on both sides as a way of easing the tension between their countries.[11] Burundi, Rwanda, and Zaire also decided to set up a tripartite standing committee to suggest appropriate measures to help refugees return to their countries of origin in accordance with the Geneva Convention on refugees; to consult regularly on problems of common interest; and to communicate to one another all information relating to the maintenance of security in their three states.

When hostilities erupted again in 1978, it was decided at the Khartoum Summit that Tanzania and Zaire should become involved in helping to effect a reconciliation between the adversaries. Tanzania and Zaire did succeed in procuring an agreement between the parties, which was similar to the former agreement, and which incorporated the essential elements of the OAU Convention on Refugees. As members of the commission that drew up the convention, Rwanda and Burundi had no problem in reaching a mutual understanding on the refugee issue, in line with the principles of that convention. Since they arrived at this mutual understanding, there has not been any major clash between the two countries, even though intermittent outbreaks of internal unrest still continue.

In Rwanda, for instance, the civil insurrection which broke out in October 1990 went out of hand in 1994 when the Hutus carried an orchestrated massacre of Tutsis, following the plane crash in which the country's Hutu President died. This massacre added fuel to the struggle by the Tutsi-dominated Rwanda Patriotic Front (RPF) to oust the government. The sacking of the government by RPF forces led to mass exodus of Hutu into neighbouring countries to escape possible Tutsi retaliation.

Burundi, whose president also died in the same plane crash, also witnessed the outbreak of ethnic violence. The violence that took place in the country in 1994 was, however, of a lesser degree than that of Rwanda. Although no inter-state hostilities took place as a result, the crisis succeeded in aggravating the refugee problem in the sub-region; so much so, that neighbouring countries, especially Zaire and Tanzania, had to complain loudly about their inability to cope. Despite the general frustration with the refugee situation, neither Rwanda nor Burundi, nor any of the neighbouring countries took advantage of the unprecedented influx of refugees to resort to hostile action against its neighbours, or provoke the type of inter-state hostilities the sub-region witnessed between 1963 and 1978. Evidently, there was mutual commitment by all the affected parties to adhere to the principles of the OAU convention on Refugees.

The convention, apart from its humanitarian consideration, reflected the organisation's primary concern for harmonious relationships among its member states. The convention thus went further than the UN convention on refugees in trying to eliminate the conflict potential of the refugee problem. In addition to the principles noted above, the OAU convention made it virtually obligatory for member states to grant asylum to persons in need. As stated in Article II, "no person shall be subjected by a member-state to measures such as rejection at the frontier, return or expulsion which would compel him to return or remain in a territory where his life, physical integrity or liberty would be threatened".

No attempt was made to include, as is the case with the UN convention, the proviso that refugees can be denied admission for "overriding reasons of national security." The OAU sought to entrench the principle of obligatory acceptance of refugees as an inter-state norm in Africa, thereby ensuring that no state is blamed simply for accepting refugees. At the same time, the OAU Convention on Refugees imposed obligations on the refugee to respect the laws of the host country and to desist from any action against the country of origin.

Inevitably, the OAU convention has not completely eliminated inter-state friction arising from refugee problems. Goodwill is required if the provisions of the convention are to operate as intended. However, apart from the Uganda-Tanzania conflict (discussed below), most refugee-related conflicts have imposed minor strains rather than produced ruptures in the relationships between the affected states.

Also instrumental to the relatively harmonious relationship existing between Rwanda and Burundi are the integrative steps that have been taken by the countries in the sub-region. One such measure is the move in the late 1960s to form the Economic Community of the Great Lakes Countries (CEPGL), a move which could help the two tiny countries to overcome the economic disability that their small sizes inflict. Another complementary development is the formation of a tripartite security commission in January 1989 by the two countries and Zaire with the aim of guaranteeing their security against aggression and possible attempts at their subversion.[12] These developments, provided that they do not remain mere paper agreements, seem certain to help in promoting mutual trust and understanding between these neighbouring countries.

Overall, the OAU's decision to go into the refugee issue which was at the root of the conflict between Rwanda and Burundi is a positive attempt at problem solving. Admittedly, a lasting solution is yet to be found for the endemic internal ethnic problems in both countries. Nevertheless, OAU's efforts have paid off to a considerable degree in the sense that the antagonism between Rwanda and Burundi that normally accompanied their internal conflicts has been conspicuously absent in their latest internal unrest.

The Uganda-Tanzania Conflict (1972-1979)

Background

Although the roots of the Uganda-Tanzania conflict can be traced to refugee problems engendered by the overthrow of the government of Milton Obote in Uganda, the conflict later expanded to involve disagreements on their common borders and system/ideological factors. Until January 1971, when President Obote was overthrown by his chief of defence staff, General Idi Amin, Uganda and Tanzania enjoyed the best of relations. Just before his overthrow, Milton Obote had followed President Julius Nyerere of Tanzania in embracing socialism. This ideological compatibility, strengthened by a personal friendship between the two leaders, made Tanzania the obvious choice as a place of refuge for the ousted Obote and his close associates.

From their refuge in Tanzania, the former Ugandan leader and his followers did not commit themselves to good behaviour as prescribed in the OAU Convention on Refugees. Rather, they used Tanzania as a base for subversive activities against President Idi Amin's government. The Tanzanian government did not see it fit to restrict the activities of Obote and his men. In fact, Nyerere, who had no liking for military regimes, openly condemned Idi Amin's coup and refused to accord the new Ugandan government any legitimacy.

Uganda wanted Obote to be repatriated to that country, or at least expelled from Tanzania – a demand to which Tanzania was not prepared to accede. The conflict, which began with a radio and press war, escalated into open hostilities in September 1972, when Amin alleged an Israeli/Tanzania-assisted invasion of his country by pro-Obote elements and retaliated by ordering the Ugandan air force to bomb border villages in Tanzania. During the course of the conflict, Amin tried to occupy and claim the Kagera Salient in Tanzania, some 710 square miles of territory, which he claimed had been part of Uganda in pre-colonial times.

The OAU's Response

The initial OAU response when the conflict erupted in September 1972 was through its Secretary-General, who appealed to the parties to exercise restraint and seek a peaceful solution to their conflict in accordance with the spirit of the OAU Charter. Similar appeals for restraint also came from a number of African leaders. It was through the good offices of President Siad Barre of Somalia that Uganda and Tanzania signed a cease-fire agreement on October 5, 1972. Under the agreement, which came to be known as the Mogadishu Peace Agreement, the two countries undertook to withdraw their troops from each other's territory and desist from allowing their territories to be used as bases for subversive activities against each other. Somalia provided an observer team to monitor the troop withdrawals.

Because no arrangement was made to monitor the cease-fire after the withdrawal of troops, hostilities soon flared up again. This resulted in yet another agreement, concluded on May 25, 1973, under the good offices of Emperor Haile Selassie of Ethiopia. Under the new agreement, known as the Addis Ababa Accord, Uganda and Tanzania pledged to resolve their differences through peaceful means. However, no action was taken to try and resolve the fundamental issues involved in the conflict, neither was any neutral force deployed to create a buffer between the hostile parties. Relations between the two countries therefore remained strained, with border clashes occurring sporadically.

When these clashes erupted into a major war in October 1978, the OAU's action came through its current chairman, President Jafar Nimeiri of the Sudan. Accompanied by the OAU Secretary-General, he travelled to Kampala and Dar-es-Salaam to appeal personally to the two leaders, Idi Amin and Julius Nyerere, to halt the fighting. By this time, the Ugandan leader had declared that he was extending his country's borders to include the Kagera Salient in Tanzania and ordered his forces to occupy the area. The OAU chairman was unable to persuade the two countries to stop fighting.

Idi Amin said his troops would stop fighting only after

Tanzania had stopped interfering in his country's internal affairs and withdrawn its forces from the border. Nyerere wanted the OAU to publicly condemn Uganda as the aggressor and compel it to withdraw its troops from Tanzania territory. He declared he would consider a cease-fire only after Uganda had renounced all claims to the territory its troops had occupied and promised to pay compensation for the destruction of property and the loss of life caused by Ugandan forces.

As the fighting intensified, the nine-member ad hoc committee on inter-African disputes, established by the 14th Summit of the OAU in Libreville in July 1977, was activated to mediate the conflict. Nigeria chaired the committee and its members included the Central African Republic, Gabon, Gambia, Madagascar, Togo, Tunisia, Zaire and Zambia. The committee arranged a reconciliation meeting to take place in Nairobi, Kenya, on February 21, 1978, which was reluctantly attended by Tanzania and willingly by Uganda. By this time, the fortunes of the war had turned in favour of Tanzania, which had regained all of its territory and was now pushing deep into Uganda.

The delegations of the two countries to the meeting were led by their foreign ministers. They both restated the positions of their respective governments. After four days of deliberations, the committee made the following recommendations: an immediate and total cease-fire by both parties; the unequivocal renunciation of territorial claims; the withdrawal of forces behind their internationally recognised borders; respect for the principles of non-interference in the internal affairs of member states; respect for the sovereignty and territorial integrity of states as embodied in the OAU Charter; and the reaffirmation of the Mogadishu Peace Agreement and the Addis Ababa Accord by both parties. The committee also recommended that a control commission be set up to supervise the cease-fire and the withdrawal of forces. The issue of compensation for war damages was to be referred to the heads of state for their consideration.

After making its recommendations, the committee immediately dispatched missions to Kampala and Dar-es-Salaam to convey its recommendations to Amin and Nyerere. The two missions, which left on February 25, 1979, returned that same day.

Uganda accepted the recommendations of the committee, but Tanzania insisted on its demand for OAU condemnation of Uganda as a precondition for the acceptance of the committee's recommendations. A second mission sent by the committee to Dar-es-Salaam to convey Uganda's written acceptance of the committee's recommendations, including the renunciation of the territorial claims against Tanzania, did not persuade the Tanzanian leader. He continued with the prosecution of the war.

Unable to effect a cease-fire, the OAU ad hoc committee accepted its failure and simply noted that it has done everything possible to bring about an end to the hostilities between the two countries. The committee decided to submit its final report to the Secretary-General for transmission to the current chairman of the OAU. Ultimately, the Uganda-Tanzania conflict was settled on the battlefield, with Amin defeated and ousted from power.

The conflict was then a failure as far as the OAU conflict management efforts were concerned. Why had it failed? Certainly, an important factor was the personal animosity between Nyerere and Amin and the fact that at no time were both sides prepared to compromise. Once his forces had overturned early Ugandan successes, Nyerere was determined to press on with the war until Amin acceded to his demands or was removed from power. The conflict did not reach, in William Zartman's phrase, a "mutual hurting stalemate", and was thus never "ripe for resolution."[13] With the escalation of the conflict into open warfare, and the OAU lacking any means for enforcement action, a "mutual hurting stalemate" could have aided OAU's efforts to bring the parties to the negotiating table.

However, had the OAU acted differently in the period between 1973 and 1978 it might have been able to prevent the conflict escalating to a level at which a win-win solution was no longer feasible in the face of one or another side's determination to press for a win-lose outcome. Two weaknesses in the OAU's conflict management efforts can be pin-pointed. The first was the inability of the organisation to put in place an effective monitoring force to ensure compliance with agreements and to act as a buffer between the hostile parties after the troop disengagement of May 1973. The presence of such a neutral force along the Ugandan-

Tanzanian border could also have curtailed frequent incidents and thus enhanced the OAU's diplomatic efforts to settle the conflict. This inability to organise peace-keeping forces to monitor cease-fires and troop disengagement has undermined the conflict management efforts of the organisation on more than one occasion.

The second failing in the OAU's response to the Uganda-Tanzania conflict (and also a failing that has undercut the organisation's work on several occasions) was its inability to sustain a process of negotiation between the parties after the cease-fire agreements had been reached. The mediation technique employed by the ad hoc committee, which enjoins the parties in conflict to state their cases, after which the committee makes its recommendations, does little to foster the harmonisation of the interests of the parties in conflict. This technique is not very different from the judicial method, which does not provide ample opportunity for the parties in conflict to iron out their differences through direct negotiations. Apparently sensing the lack of opportunity for direct bargaining during these ad hoc meetings, both Uganda and Tanzania resorted to setting preconditions for their participation.

The Chadian Conflict (1966-1990)

Background

The conflict in Chad began as a revolt by an alienated Muslim North against the Central government, which was dominated by the Westernised Christian South. Later, the conflict degenerated into a free-for-all struggle by several nationalist factions from both the North and the South for control of the Central government in N'djamena. While the conflict was thus essentially a system/ideological conflict, it was compounded by very considerable external involvement in support of various factions considered likely to safeguard the interests of the respective interventionists.

The territory that come to be known as Chad was a French creation. It is made up of people of diverse nationalities and cultures spreading over half a million square miles and speaking almost 200 local languages and dialects. After fashioning a state out of this diversity, France made no attempt at national integration in Chad. The country's colonial policy of assimilation had some success in the South, but it never took root in the north, which had been Islamised before the imposition of colonial rule. In effect, the North refused to be Westernised and held on to its Arabic and Islamic culture.

At independence, the departing French colonial rulers transferred power to a government dominated by the Westernised and better-educated Southerners, with Francois (later Ngarta) Tombalbaye as president. Tombalbaye's government did not attempt to bridge the gap between South and North. The situation worsened after January 19, 1962, when Tombalbaye dissolved all political parties except his own, i.e., the Parti Progressiste Tchadien (PPT). Deprived of effective participation in the government, opposition groups from the North in 1966 formed the Front National de Liberation du Tchad (FROLINAT) in the Sudan under the leadership of Ibrahim Abatcha. On the death of Abatcha in 1968, Abba Siddick took over the leadership of FROLINAT. Siddick later lost the leadership of FROLINAT to its military section, and escaped from the Front's base in Tripoli to seek refuge in Algiers. From there, he established what he called the Political Bureau of FROLINAT.

The formation of FROLINAT marked the beginning of an organised-armed rebellion against the Tombalbaye government. By 1968, the war was so intense that Tombalbaye had to request French intervention to save his country from total disintegration. The French military rescue mission was accompanied by a reform package and French administrators to ensure that the reforms were carried out. Apart from helping to alleviate inter-ethnic friction for a brief period, the reconciliation measures belatedly embarked upon by Tombalbaye were ineffectual. On April 13, 1975, he was killed in a military coup staged by Southern officers, many of whom he had alienated. General Felix Malloum was released from detention to head the new military government.

FROLINAT had meanwhile splintered into as many as nine factions, and the North-South division had ceased to be a valid frame of reference for identifying either insurgents or supporters of the Chadian central government. At its peak, the Chadian civil war involved eleven factions. These included:

- Forces Armies Tchadiennes (FAT), led by Felix Malloum and Wadal Abdelkader Kamougue;
- Forces Armies Populaires (FAP), led by Goukouni Weddeye (also spelled Oueddei);
- Forces Armies du Nord (FAN), led by Hissene Habre;
- Mouvement Populaire pour la Liberation du Tchad (MPLT), led by Aboubakar Mahamet Abderamane;
- Forces Populaires de Liberation (FPL), led by Mahamet Abba;
- Conseil Democratique Revolutionaire (CDR), led by Ahmat Acyl;
- FROLINAT Originel, led by Abba Siddick;
- Forces Armies Occidentales (FAO), led by Moussa Medela;
- FROLINAT Fondamental, led by Hadjaro Sanoussi;
- Volcan, led by Abdoulaye Adam Dana; and
- Union Nationale Democratique (UND), formed by a group of intellectual pacifists.

Efforts by Malloum to woo the various factions into joining him in a government of national unity proved largely unsuccessful. A marriage of convenience with Habre's FAN lasted only from August 1978 to February 1979, when Habre accused Malloum of discrimination against the people of the north and launched a war against the government of which he was a part. The government forces (FAT) under the supreme authority of Malloum were no match for Habre's more mobile and aggressive FAN. The confusion created by the fighting left N'djamena paralysed and without effective authority. It was at this point that neighbouring countries headed by Nigeria took the initiative to bring the parties together in an attempt to settle their differences.

The OAU's Response

The OAU's involvement in the Chadian conflict started in an

indirect manner via two channels. One has to do with mediation between Libya and Chad over Libyan involvement in the conflict, while the second was more or less a follow-up to the initiative of some of its members, led by Nigeria. Libya had been one of the chief financial supporters of FROLINAT since its inception. When the movement splintered, Libya continued to support some factions, particularly, those that seemed likely to accept Libya's take-over of the Aouzou Strip, a region of 114,000 square kilometres in the extreme north of Chad believed to be rich in uranium and manganese. Libya moved its troops into the region in 1973 and laid claim to it by virtue of a treaty signed between the Vichy regime in France and Italy in 1943. None of the Chadian factions accepted the Libyan annexation of the Aouzou strip. In fact, both Habre and Goukouni Weddeye, as leaders of FROLINAT, had at times lost the backing of Libya for refusing to recognise the take-over.

It was at the Libreville Summit in July 1977 that the Chadian issue was brought before the OAU, when Malloum accused Libya of interfering in Chad's internal affairs by supporting various FROLINAT factions fighting against his government. He also accused Libya of occupying part of Chadian territory (the Aouzou Strip) since 1973. After listening to the response from the Libyan foreign minister, Ali Abdel Salam El-Traiki, the OAU Assembly of Heads of State and Government decided to establish an ad hoc committee made up of Algeria, Cameroon, Gabon, Mozambique, Nigeria and Senegal, with Gabon's leader as chairman. Part of the committee's terms of reference was "to find the ways and means likely to lead to the satisfactory solution of the serious problem and report to the Assembly of Heads of State and Government."[14]

The ad hoc committee met in August 1977 and set up a sub-committee of experts (made up of jurists and cartographers) to study the documents submitted by the two parties, to visit the capitals of the countries as well as the disputed area, and to report back to the committee. Meanwhile, the committee appealed to both countries to refrain from taking any action that was likely to impede the committee's work or worsen the situation. The sub-committee was scheduled to meet in January 1978, but could not do so because of a poor response from its members. Other scheduled meetings failed to take place for similar reasons. Apparently, the members were busy with more pressing national issues. However, as a result of the joint efforts of the heads of state of Nigeria and Sudan, the leaders of the parties in conflict met in February 1978 at Sebha in Libya and signed an agreement by which they undertook to seek a negotiated settlement to the dispute.

This commitment by the leaders of Libya and Chad was not followed by practical action. The entire process was complicated by the lack of progress in the settlement of the civil war. Habre's seizure of power had placed a further obstacle in the way of negotiations because of the antagonism between him and the Libyan leader, Muammar Gaddafi. A number of meetings took place at the foreign minister's level, but they were unproductive. Not until 1989 did Habre and Gaddafi meet, at a summit in Bamako, which led to the conclusion of the Algiers Framework Agreement on August 31, 1989. Under Article 6 of the agreement, the contracting parties agreed to a peaceful and political resolution of their territorial dispute, failing which they would refer the matter to the ICJ in the Hague. On September 1, 1990, having failed to reach a political solution, the parties referred the matter to the ICJ.[15]

As for the war that was raging between FROLINAT and the government of Malloum, very little was achieved by the ad hoc committee. At one point, in March 1978, Malloum secured the co-operation of Libya to work out a cease-fire agreement with FROLINAT, at conferences in Sebha and Benghazi in Libya. The cease-fire agreement, like many others that followed, collapsed almost immediately after its signing. The hope that the agreement would form the basis for a unified government that would include both Habre and Weddeye, never materialised, as Malloum refused to agree to Weddeye's demand that all French troops be withdrawn.

The initial efforts to get the opposing parties to the negotiating table did not involve the direct participation of the OAU. The Organisation merely rubber-stamped the initiative of Nigeria. Four peace conferences were held under Nigeria's auspices within six months between March and August 1979. The first one took place in Kano in March 1979. It was attended by representatives of four Chadian factions – FAT, FAP, FAN, and MPLT – as well as countries bordering Chad – Cameroon, Niger, Libya and Sudan. The conference was presided over by Nigeria's General Shehu Yar' Adua.

After five days of intensive negotiations, the parties signed a peace accord on March 16, 1979, with the following provisions:

- A general cease-fire in Chad and the establishment of a neutral peace-keeping force to be provided by Nigeria.
- The setting up of an independent monitoring commission under the chairmanship of Nigeria and comprising delegates from the countries attending the Kano conference and from representatives of the Chadian factions.
- The establishment of a transitional government of national union to prepare a programme leading to the installation of a freely elected government composed of all factions with its leader elected by them.
- The demilitarisation of N'djamena to a radius of 100 kilometres.
- A general amnesty for political prisoners and hostages and the release of prisoners of war, with the pardon extending also to those living in exile.
- The dissolution of all political organisations and the gradual integration of military factions into the national army.[16]

The agreement, known as the Kano Accord, did not lead to a lasting settlement. On March 23, 1979, Malloum and Habre resigned to pave the way for the establishment of a Provisional State Council of eight members – two from each of the four factions that signed the Kano Accord. Weddeye was appointed president of the Provisional Council. The first contingent of Nigerian troops arrived in Chad in late March 1979; Nigeria's total troop commitment for peace-keeping in Chad, before the implementation of the other provisions of the Kano Accord went sour, was about 800.

Several of the tasks assigned to the peace-keeping force, such as ensuring the freedom of movement throughout Chad, were overly ambitious, given the vast territory to cover and the numerous Chadian armed factions scattered all over the country. After securing some measure of success in bringing order to N'djamena, the operation hit a snag when the neutral force tried to get the factional troops and guerrilla elements to pull out from the demilitarised zone. The peace-keepers could not even secure the full co-operation of the leaders of the factions that were signatories to the accord; still less the compliance of factions that had not been represented at Kano. In fact, some of them instigated the population against the neutral force, which they branded as an occupation force.

Amid this confusing situation, Nigeria convened the second Kano Conference in April 1979, in an attempt to get the parties to work out the details of the agreement and practical measures to be taken towards its implementation. Representatives of five more factions, namely, FROLINAT Originel, FROLINAT Fondamental, Volcan, FPL, and CDR, attended the conference. Weddeye and Habre refused to recognise the five new factions and withdrew from the meeting. The Conference could not therefore achieve much. Nonetheless, it decided to set up a fact-finding mission to be sent to Chad to verify the relative strength of the four parties and the other factions that wished to be signatories to the Kano Accord.

Meanwhile, Habre's FAN and Weddeye's FAP decided to come to an agreement with FAT, now led by Kamaougue after the departure of Malloum, to form a government from which they planned to exclude those factions they felt were dependent on foreign government or lacking in sufficient domestic support. Consequently, Lol Mohamed Shawa, a member of the MPLT, became president of the new Government of National Unity (GUNT), while Kamaougue became vice-president. Kamaougue later defected and was replaced by General Negue Djogo, an officer from the South who had remained in the capital while most southerners left for fear of their safety. A 30-member ministerial council was established, with 10 seats being reserved for Southerners. In reality, however, effective power was in the hands of Weddeye and Habre.

The arrangement did not last, as those factions left out revolted against the new government. Encouraged by the refusal of Nigeria and Libya, the leading peace brokers in Chad, to recognise the new government, these other factions intensified the war against the new government. Between May 26 and 27, 1979, Nigeria, in collaboration with Libya, hosted another Conference, which brought together all the factions ranged against the new government in Chad. The four factions earlier represented in the nominal government refused to send representatives. Also present at this meeting was the Central African Republic, another Chadian neighbour that had not been represented at the previous meetings.

At the end of the meeting, a communiqué was issued that called for the dissolution of the Habre-Weddeye government and the establishment of a true government of national unity by June 25, 1979. Nigeria followed this up by ensuring effective international isolation of the government. It also imposed an economic boycott and cut off oil supplies to the landlocked territory. The Chadian government responded with a demand that Nigeria should withdraw its "occupation force". The frustrated peace-keeping force was thus withdrawn between June 4 and 5, 1979.[17]

It was shortly thereafter, at the Monrovia Summit of July 1979, that the OAU addressed itself fully to the civil strife in Chad. It endorsed Nigeria's efforts as a mediator in the conflict and refused to seat the delegation of the new government. The summit also decided to sponsor a fourth conciliatory meeting of all Chadian factions in Lagos in August 1979. And for the first time, it mandated the OAU Secretary-General, Edem Kodjo, to negotiate and supervise a cease-fire in Chad. Faced with effective isolation and economic strangulation, the leaders of the four factions represented in the government in Chad were now eager to attend the proposed conference.

The conference opened in Lagos on August 14, 1979, with all 11 Chadian factions participating. Also present were delegates from neighbouring countries and representatives from Benin, Congo, and Senegal. After a week of intensive negotiations, what came to be known as the Lagos Accord was signed on August 21, 1979. The Lagos Accord incorporated many of the elements of the Kano Accord. It called for an immediate cease-fire, the demilitarisation of N'djamena and its environs, the release of political prisoners, a general amnesty for political exiles, and the establishment of a broad-based transitional government under the presidency of Weddeye and with Kamougue as Vice-President to prepare for elections within 18 months. The accord made provision for an independent monitoring commission to be headed by the OAU Secretary-General or his representative to supervise the cease-fire. There was also provision for a neutral force to be made up of contingents from countries not bordering on Chad. It was subsequently agreed that Benin, Congo, and Guinea would provide the neutral force. Finally, the Accord called for the withdrawal of French troops, noting that "the continued presence of French soldiers is an impediment to a lasting solution of the problem in the country."[18]

The OAU became fully involved in the Chadian conflict from this time onwards, with the Secretary-General as the chairman of the monitoring commission, which comprised representatives of neighbouring states and Liberia. The Transitional Government of National Unity (GUNT) was inaugurated on November 11, 1979, with the leaders of all the Chadian factions represented and Habre as defence minister. However, what appeared to be a successful reconciliation of all the Chadian factions was short-lived. The projected neutral force did not materialise. No detailed plans were worked-out for the deployment and command of the force. Only the Congolese contingent of 500 troops made an appearance in Chad on January 18, 1980. They remained sequestered in barracks until they were evacuated by the French between March 30 and April 3, 1980.

In the absence of any effective monitoring mechanism, it was not surprising that the peace settlement could not hold. By the middle of March, war had broken out again, with Habre's faction fighting against the other factions that constituted the GUNT. Meanwhile, no fresh initiative came from the OAU, except for reiterations at various meetings of its call for the implementation of the Lagos Accord. The OAU set up an ad hoc committee, comprising Guinea, Nigeria and Togo, with President Senghor of Senegal as chairman, to organise a cease-fire in Chad and establish a budget to finance peace-keeping efforts there. The Council of Ministers subsequently estimated the budget of U.S $60 million. None of these plans materialised by the time of the next OAU Summit in Freetown, Sierra Leone, in July 1980.

At the Freetown Summit, the OAU reaffirmed the validity of the Lagos Accord as the basis for the settlement of the Chadian conflict. It requested African states to provide peace-keeping forces at their own expense, with the understanding, that logistic and operational costs would be met later from voluntary contributions by member-states. It held out the possibility of seeking UN assistance in the event of a failure to raise the necessary funds to service the peace-keeping operation from among its members. Again, none of this was put into effect. Fresh efforts by the ad hoc committee and the current chairman, President Siaka Stevens of Sierra Leone, to organise a cease-fire failed, and the situation in Chad continued to deteriorate.

Under intense pressure from Habre's better organised forces, Weddeye sought help first from Nigeria and then from Libya, to save the GUNT. Libya's positive response led to the decisive defeat of Habre's forces and the temporary stabilisation of the GUNT. Even though Libya's intervention helped to consolidate the OAU-backed settlement in Chad, the announcement of a planned merger between Chad and Libya provoked negative responses from other OAU members. Consequently, the OAU's attention centred now more on how to get the Libyan troops out of Chad than on how to stabilise the GUNT. Anti-Libya forces both within the organisation (Egypt, Nigeria and Sudan) and outside (the United States, France, and Great Britain) goaded on the OAU.

Libyan intervention had led to the decisive defeat of one party and had thereby presented the OAU with the opportunity to conclude a meaningful and binding negotiated settlement of the conflict. Instead, anti-Libya sentiment and the promise of resource support from the United States, France, and Britain, led the OAU to attempt a peace-keeping operation for which it had neither the funds nor the administrative capacity to support.

The OAU ad hoc committee on Chad met in Lome on January

14, 1981, to consider developments in Chad. In a nine-point communiqué, the committee condemned the reported merger plan between Libya and Chad as violating the spirit and letter of the 1979 Lagos Accord. It then called on all foreign powers to withdraw their troops and military personnel from Chad. It also recommended the urgent dispatch of OAU peace-keeping forces to Chad, to be composed of troops from the Congo, Guinea, and Togo. It declared that any election in Chad not conducted under the auspices of the OAU would be invalid, and mandated the OAU Secretary-General to organise a free and fair election in the country by the end of April 1981.[19]

Obviously, little thought had been given to the financial, logistic, and other problems involved, and nothing was done to implement the committee's decision before the next OAU Summit in Nairobi. When the Nairobi Summit met between June 24 and 27, 1981, it simply reaffirmed the earlier decisions embodied in the Lagos Accord and the Lome communiqué to dispatch a peace-keeping force to Chad, with the recommendation that the current chairman should seek UN assistance for the establishment and operation of the force. The function of the peace-keeping force, as stated in the summit resolution, would be "to maintain security and defence of the State of Chad until the formation of a Chadian national integrated army."[20] The OAU current chairman, President Arap Moi of Kenya was to contact countries that would be willing to contribute troops to the proposed force. Initially, Algeria, Togo, Madagascar, Benin, Guinea, Nigeria, Senegal and Zaire agreed to contribute troops, though in the end only the latter five were asked to send troops to be commanded by Nigeria's Major General G.O. Ejiga. At the preliminary meeting of the troop-contributing countries in Lagos, in November 1981, they assigned responsibilities among themselves.

Despite its decision to plunge into peace-keeping in Chad, the OAU clearly lacked the funds to service the operation. The Monrovia Summit of July 1979 had decided to set up an assistance fund for the rehabilitation of the victims of the Chadian civil war and requested all OAU members to contribute U.S $50,000 each. By the time the OAU ad hoc committee met in Nairobi to approve the operational plan of the troop-contributing countries, only

$400,000 had been paid into the fund. Out of this, $275,000 had been transferred directly to the Chadian government, and no decision was taken to ask member states to make additional contributions toward the operational costs of the peace-keeping force. This meant that the OAU had only a $125,000 operational fund for Chad in hand, with the unlikely possibility of raising another $2.1 million if all its members paid the original levy of $50,000. Such a sum of money was woefully inadequate for an operation that was anticipated to cost $192 million in its first year.[21]

Apparently, the OAU was relying substantially on external funding of the operation. The ad hoc committee was informed that the United States, Great Britain, and France had indicated that they would help by providing funds and military equipment to support the troops in Chad. The OAU was to be disappointed when the three countries failed to make good their promises. What the OAU did not realise was that the interest of these three countries in peace-keeping in Chad was limited to seeing the withdrawal of Libyan troops. After achieving that goal, the fate of the OAU was of little concern to them. It is not surprising that these same powers were instrumental in providing the resources that enabled Habre to fight his way back to power in Chad on June 7, 1982 – a development which became a source of embarrassment to the OAU.

To pave the way for the deployment of the OAU peace-keeping force, Libya rapidly withdrew all its troops and equipment. Because the OAU troops did not immediately replace the departing Libyan troops, a vacuum was created which Habre was quick to exploit. He reactivated his force and launched another bid for power. Driven by a sense of urgency, the OAU peace-keeping force moved into Chad, but not without problems

Not all the states fulfilled their pledges to send troops. The battalion from Benin, which was to take care of communications, could not depart for Chad because the troops had no military uniforms or equipment. The government of Guinea was no longer willing to send its battalion because it disapproved of the idea of the operations being financed by foreign powers. Of the projected 5,000 troops, only 3,300 were actually deployed to key positions in Chad by January 1982. These were made up of 2,000 from

Nigeria, 700 from Zaire, and 600 from Senegal. The Zairean battalion, which was to take care of the medical needs of the troops, arrived in Chad with doctors but without any drugs or medical equipment. With no resource support from the OAU, Nigeria had to shoulder the extra burden of providing most of the needs of the troops, including drugs, medical equipment, food and even water, apart from communications services.[22]

The arrangement that the OAU would take over the cost of the operation one month after the arrival of the forces in Chad did not materialise. The contingents had to rely on their respective governments for uniforms, arms, allowances and other necessities, thereby putting them under the considerable influence of their respective home governments. Even the OAU Secretary-General's special representative, Gebre-Egziaber Dawit, who was expected to monitor the operation, arrived in Chad without any funds to establish his office. He had to operate from his hotel room and for the first two months of his stay in N'djamena, had to depend wholly on the United Nations Development Programme (UNDP) for secretarial services and communications facilities. Although he was sent a skeletal staff of his own during the third month, his other conditions remained the same.[23]

Efforts by the OAU to secure UN financial and other assistance for the Chadian peace-keeping operation were not successful.[24] The UN Security Council was not prepared to commit itself to extensive financial involvement in a peace-keeping operation over which it had no control. The furthest the Security Council went in responding to the needs of the OAU was to adopt a resolution calling on the UN Secretary-General to establish a fund for assistance to the OAU force in Chad, "to be supplied by voluntary contributions."[25] There is no record that the OAU received any funds from the United Nations throughout the entire Chadian operation.

With the victorious entry of Habre's forces into N'djamena on June 7, 1982, the OAU accepted the failure of its peace-keeping mission in Chad and decided to withdraw the troops. That the peace-keeping force could not prevent the advance of Habre's forces was partly due to the nature of the mandate given to the peace-keeping mission, which was, to maintain absolute neutrality in the internal conflict. In December 1981, the OAU Secretary-General explained that the force was "to maintain peace and safeguard Chad's security without fighting against other factions."[26] However, the force had no chance of maintaining peace and safeguarding security unless it was prepared to intervene to prevent the fighting or create a security zone between the opposing sides.

Weddeye's GUNT had expected that the OAU force would at least help to keep Habre's forces at bay. When, on February 10 and 11, 1982, the OAU current Chairman convened another meeting of the standing committee in Nairobi at Summit level, Weddeye tried unsuccessfully to talk the OAU out of its neutral position. When he could not, he withdrew and accused the OAU of betrayal. At the end of the meeting, the committee adopted a new agenda for peace in Chad in which it called on the Chadian factions to:

- embark on a cease-fire by midnight of February 28, 1982;
- commence negotiations for national reconciliation under the auspices of the OAU Standing Committee, in an African country to be determined, as from March 15, 1982;
- draft and adopt a provisional constitution from April 1-30, 1982;
- organise legislative and presidential elections between May 1 and June 30, 1982 and install the new institutions under the auspices of the OAU; and
- terminate the mandate and effect the withdrawal of the inter-African force by June 30, 1982.[27]

Like the OAU's previous resolutions, this one had no practical effect. The conflict was temporarily settled by Habre's victory over Weddeye's GUNT. Weddeye, who fled into Cameroon, soon after, reorganised his forces and launched a counter-attack. By July 1983, his forces were in effective control of the northern third of Chad. But Habre was able to hold on until December 1990, when he was overthrown by Idris Deby who led a coalition of Chadian factions against him. Whether or not Chad will henceforth enjoy a lasting peace will depend on the extent to which Deby is able to bring all the Chadian factions together to work out a truly inclusive and representative democratic government. So far (as at 1995), Deby has been able to contain the situation and ensure some measure of stability in Chad.

Chad was the first conflict in which the OAU tried to organise a peace-keeping force. As it turned out, the force deployed in Chad was an OAU force only in name. With the OAU, unable to give the peace-keepers the necessary resource and administrative support, the mission fell under the control of the individual troop-contributing countries and their foreign backers. The experience of the OAU in Chad shows that some measure of coercive intervention on the part of the third-party intervenor may be necessary in getting the parties to the negotiating table. This method worked when it came to getting the parties to the negotiating table in Lagos in August 1979, at which time they concluded the Lagos Accord. The absence of an adequate monitoring mechanism and of any follow-up action to help create a truly representative democratic government, undermined the gains of the Lagos Accord. As was noted earlier, the OAU also failed to exploit the opportunity offered at the end of 1980 by Libya's coercive intervention; the pause in the conflict benefited only the combatants, who used it to prepare for renewed hostilities.

The OAU Chadian experience also demonstrates the frustration that can arise when an organisation embarks on a peace-keeping operation without having made adequate preparation for it. Not surprising, the OAU's failure in Chad seems to have left the organisation wary of peace-keeping. Thus, under its new mechanism for conflict prevention and resolution, the OAU has still neglected the desirability of drawing up contingency plans for possible future peace-keeping missions. Though this disinclination to contemplate future peace-keeping or monitoring missions may be understandable, the effectiveness of the OAU as a conflict manager is clearly reduced by the organisation's refusal to prepare for operations that cannot only contain and abate violence but also create an atmosphere in which negotiations aimed at a final resolution of the conflict can occur.

The Morocco-Western Sahara Conflict (1975-1983)

Background

The Morocco-Western Sahara Conflict is extremely complicated. Though rooted in pre-colonial times, the conflict can best be understood by an appreciation of the mineral endowment of the desert territory of some 252,120 square kilometres and a population of less than a million. The territory was, until 1975, under the colonial tutelage of Spain, and was called Spanish Sahara. Apart from its strategic importance during the period of imperialist struggle for Africa, what later generated much interest in the territory was the discovery in the Sikiel-el-Hamra and the Rio de Oro regions of large deposits of phosphate and iron ore. This discovery was largely responsible for the Spanish determination to hold on to the territory indefinitely. From 1964, Spain began to encourage the migration of large numbers of its nationals to the territory to populate it and forestall the eventual demand by the people of Western Sahara for independence.

Also attracted by the territory's rich mineral resources, were the country's three neighbours, Morocco, Mauritania, and Algeria. Whereas both Morocco and Mauritania had territorial designs on Western Sahara, Algeria was interested in maintaining the independence of the territory, albeit under Algerian influence.

Mauritania, itself a victim of Morocco's territorial ambitions, pursued its interest in Western Sahara, and even colluded with Morocco and Spain in 1975 in a planned partition of the territory. Mauritania was to abandon its claim on August 5, 1979, unable to bear any longer the economic costs of sustaining the war (by 1977, the country was spending about 60 percent of its budget on defence).

It was, however, a different matter for Morocco, a country which was eager to redress the reduction in its territory during the European partition of Africa, and which coveted the resources of the Western Sahara. Morocco, like Western Sahara, accounts for a substantial percentage of the world's phosphate production. The mineral is the country's leading foreign exchange earner, and a number of phosphate-derivative industries have been developed in Morocco and are still being expanded. In 1990, the country's export of phosphate acid increased by 116.8 percent to reach 2 million tons, making Morocco the world's major exporter of the product, accounting for about 42 percent of the world market and pushing the United States into the second place.[28]

A take-over of Western Sahara would enable Morocco not only to check the adverse effect which increased phosphate mining in Western Sahara could have on the Moroccan economy, but also to gain a monopoly of the product, thus putting the country in a position to dictate the price of the product in the world market. The annexation of Western Sahara would also give Morocco complete control over the iron fields of Western Sahara.

Morocco's designs on Western Sahara first became evident during the 1960s, when the people of Western Sahara started agitating for independence. While paying lip service to the application of the principle of self-determination, Moroccan leaders sought to persuade the people of Western Sahara to opt for merger with the Kingdom of Morocco. When it became apparent that this was not going to work-out, Morocco pressured Spain not to grant Western Sahara independence, but to surrender the territory to the joint administration of Morocco and Mauritania.

What amounted to a sell-out of Western Sahara by Spain took place in Madrid on November 14, 1975, when Spain signed a tripartite agreement with Morocco and Mauritania, in which Spain agreed to withdraw from Western Sahara in 1976 and transfer the territory to a joint Morocco-Mauritania administration. Under the agreement, Spain was to retain a 35 percent interest in the Bu-Cra phosphate mines and hand over the remaining 65 percent to Morocco. Western Sahara was to be divided between Morocco and Mauritania along the 24th parallel, with each country taking over the portion adjoining its own territory. As noted above, Mauritania withdrew from this arrangement in 1979.

Before the Madrid meeting, the nationalist struggle in Western Sahara was directed essentially against Spanish colonial rule, with Morocco and Mauritania sponsoring different nationalist movements. After Madrid, most of these nationalist movements fused together to form POLISARIO, which declared Western Sahara an independent sovereign state on February 28, 1976, following the Spanish withdrawal from the territory, under the new name of Sahrawi Arab Democratic Republic (SADR). Thereafter, the conflict became a struggle by the SADR against first Morocco and Mauritania, and later just Morocco.

The OAU's Response

The OAU's involvement in the conflict between Morocco and Western Sahara started in earnest in 1976. Before then, the organisation relied on the African Group at the United Nations (i.e., Permanent Representatives of OAU member states at the UN) to mount the necessary pressure to persuade Spain and other interested parties to grant self-determination to the people of Western Sahara. In 1966, the UN General Assembly passed a resolution urging Spain to grant the people of Western Sahara their right to self-determination at the earliest possible date; the resolution was reaffirmed at subsequent meetings of the General Assembly.[29] The United Nations referred the various claims on the territory to the ICJ for an opinion as to whether the people were subject to the sovereign authority of any power prior to the Spanish colonisation. The United Nations also sent an investigative mission to the territory to ascertain the views of the people on the question of self-determination and possible merger with any of the neighbours of the territory. On October 14, 1975, the investigative mission reported that almost all the people interviewed in the territory were firmly in favour of independence and opposed to the territorial claims of Morocco and Mauritania. Two days later, on October 16, the ICJ also ruled in favour of self-determination.

The inhabitants of Western Sahara, it should be pointed out, are mainly nomadic Berbers and Arabs, who move from place to place with their cattle in search of grazing lands. They have no fixed concept of loyalty beyond their immediate group or clan. There is much truth in the comment by the Algerian spokesman at the OAU Council of Ministers in 1966 that "the people of Western Sahara are Moroccans for four months of the year, Mauritanians for four months of the year, and Algerians for the remaining four months of the year, because these tribes have no knowledge of frontiers."[30]

Morocco was unmoved by the findings of the UN investigative mission and the ruling of the ICJ. As soon as Spain vacated the territory on February 26, 1976, Morocco moved in its troops. Mauritania followed suit, occupying the area it had been allotted at Madrid. POLISARIO, which had by now announced the establishment of a military wing known as the Sahara Liberation Army, declared war on both Morocco and Mauritania. Algeria allowed POLISARIO to use its territory as a base from which to wage guerrilla war.

Meanwhile, the OAU Co-ordinating Committee for the Liberation of Africa, simply referred to as the Liberation Committee, had at a January 1979 session in Maputo, Mozambique, recommended that the OAU recognise POLISARIO as the authentic liberation movement of the people of Western Sahara. The recommendation was subsequently submitted to the 26th ordinary session of the Council of Ministers in Addis Ababa in February 1976. A day before the scheduled debate on the recommendation on February 28, POLISARIO announced the independence of the SADR. The Council of Ministers felt that the issue was thus no longer one of decolonisation, but one of recognition of a declared sovereign state, something that should be left to the individual OAU members, to decide in accordance with their national policies

By the next meeting of Council of Ministers in Port Louis, Mauritius, from June 24 to 29, 1976, a number of OAU member states had accorded the SADR formal recognition. The meeting adopted a resolution extending the OAU's "unconditional support to the just struggle of the Saharan people for the recovery of their national rights", and demanded the withdrawal of all foreign occupation forces, respect for the territorial integrity of the Western Sahara and the national sovereignty of the Saharan people."[31] The delegates of Morocco and Mauritania walked out of the meeting in protest, and 29 members out of the 48 voted for the resolution. Most of those states that did not vote for the resolution abstained, even though they opposed the Moroccan action in Western Sahara.

Morocco boycotted the July OAU summit in Port Louis,

threatening to withdraw completely from the organisation if the summit adopted the resolution. The Mauritanian president did attend the summit, where he lobbied against the resolution. To avoid dissension, the Mauritius Summit adopted an innocuous proposal that a fact-finding mission of the OAU or a joint mission of the OAU and the Arab League should be sent to the Western Sahara, and appealed to all the countries concerned to find a solution to the problem. It then deferred debate on the issue to an extraordinary session of the Assembly of Heads of State and government scheduled to meet before the end of the year.[32] Sir Seewoosagur Ramgoolam, the new chairman, was given the responsibility of implementing the Assembly's decision.

Neither the establishment of the fact-finding mission nor the extraordinary meeting of the Assembly materialised by the time of the 14th OAU summit in July 1977 in Libreville, Gabon. Although Western Sahara was on the agenda, the Assembly again avoided the issue and deferred its discussion until the holding of an extraordinary summit now proposed for the first half of October 1977. Once again, the proposed extraordinary summit did not take place, in part, because no country was prepared to provide the necessary facilities for the meeting and, in part, because of a general desire to avoid polarising the organisation on the issue.

At the 15th ordinary session of the Assembly in Khartoum in July 1978, the OAU abandoned the idea of an extraordinary session and decided to set up a five-member ad hoc *Committee of Wisemen*, comprising Presidents Sekou Toure of Guinea, Moussa Traore of Mali, Olusegun Obasanjo of Nigeria, Julius Nyerere of Tanzania, and Jaafar Nimeiri of Sudan, who had then taken over the chairmanship of the OAU.[33]

At its first meeting in November 1978, the committee created a fact-finding subcommittee, made up of the heads of state of Mali and Nigeria, to visit Algeria, Mauritania, Morocco, and Spain and consult with all the parties to the conflict, including the people of Western Sahara, with a view to restoring peace and security in the area. The OAU Secretary-General, Edem Kodjo, accompanied the two leaders in their mission to the four countries.

The subcommittee heard more or less the same old

arguments virtually everywhere it went. Morocco and Mauritania invoked ethnic and historical links in support of their claims to the territory, while Algeria was in favour of the right of the Saharan people to self-determination. Spain was also in support of self-determination and emphasised that the Madrid Agreement only effected a transfer of the administration of Western Sahara and not its sovereignty to Morocco and Mauritania. POLISARIO made a strong case for independence.

The *Committee of Wisemen* met in Khartoum in June 1979 to consider the report of the subcommittee, after which they decided to recommend to the OAU that it appoint a special committee of five OAU member states to design and supervise the organisation of a referendum in Western Sahara with the co-operation of the UN on the basis of one person, one vote. The recommendation was adopted after a heated debate at the 16th OAU summit in Monrovia, Liberia, in July 1979.[34] Morocco protested the passage of the resolution and walked out of the meeting.

The new OAU chairman, President Tolbert of Liberia, followed up the OAU decisions with a visit to Morocco and Algeria in November 1979 to consult with all the parties to the conflict and persuade them to attend the ad hoc committee meeting scheduled to take place in Monrovia in December. Despite his earlier assurances that he would attend, the Moroccan monarch boycotted that meeting because of what he described as the "hostile positions of other members". In a letter to President Tolbert, King Hassan of Morocco claimed that the presidents of Mali and Tanzania had "overlooked the most fundamental norms of honourable behaviour and impartiality which must characterise the role of arbitrator."[35]

By the time of the meeting of the ad hoc committee, Mauritania had abandoned its claim to Western Sahara. So the resolution from the meeting of the ad hoc committee was specifically directed at Morocco. The committee urged Morocco to withdraw its troops from Western Sahara and its administration from that part of the territory vacated by Mauritania. It also recommended an immediate cease-fire.[36]

Morocco was becoming increasingly isolated on the Western Sahara issue, while the SADR was gaining diplomatically. A considerable amount of politicking was now taking place within the OAU, with Morocco on the one side, and the supporters of the SADR led by Algeria on the other, assiduously courting the support of other member states. So fervent was the competition that the OAU virtually became an arena for continuing the conflict over Western Sahara. By the time of the Monrovia Summit in 1979, 15 African states besides Algeria had recognised the SADR; by the time of the 17th Summit in Freetown, Sierra Leone, in July 1980, 12 more African states had accorded the SADR diplomatic recognition. With the majority of member states recognising it, the SADR was thus technically entitled to the membership of the OAU. The issue of the admission of the SADR into the OAU preoccupied the Freetown Summit.

On the question of OAU membership, Article IV of the charter provides that "each independent African State shall be entitled to become a member of the Organisation." The processes governing admission are covered under Article XXVIII, which states:

> 1. Any independent sovereign African State may at any time notify the Secretary-General of the intention to adhere or accede to this Charter.
>
> 2. The Secretary-General shall on receipt of such notification, communicate a copy of it to all the Member States. Admission shall be decided by simple majority of the Member States. The decision of each member state shall be transmitted to the Secretary-General, who shall, upon receipt of the required number of votes, communicate the decision to the State concerned.

The Moroccan stand against the SADR's admission was based on the argument that the SADR was neither a state nor an independent entity. The Moroccan delegation cited Article XVII of the OAU Charter and called for an interpretation of the phrase "independent sovereign African State" by a vote of two-thirds of the assembly. Because the pro-SADR members were not confident of mustering a two-thirds majority, they did not force a debate on the issue. With clear divisions apparent among member states, the summit decided to avoid a debate on the issue and adopted a compromise resolution, which extended the mandate of the *Committee of Wisemen* to continue its attempt "to reconcile the parties to the conflict and find a peaceful, lasting solution to this conflict."[37]

The next meeting of the *Committee of Wisemen*, which occurred in Freetown in September, failed to achieve the desired settlement even though, for the first time, all the parties were represented. The Moroccan delegation included 10 pro-Moroccan Western Sahara nationalist groups. No meaningful negotiation took place because of Morocco's uncompromisingly negative attitude towards POLISARIO. As noted in the report of the *Committee of Wisemen*, Morocco maintained that POLISARIO did not exist and was a creation of Algeria; that the conflict was between Morocco and Algeria which was committing aggression and that there was no need to have a referendum since the people of Western Sahara had already expressed their wish to be integrated with Morocco in the traditional manner."[38]

In the face of Morocco's intransigence, the OAU *Committee of Wisemen* could only draw up its own six-point plan for the settlement of the conflict. Among other things, the plan proposed a cease-fire; the deployment of a peace-keeping force to ensure the effectiveness of the cease-fire; the confinement of the armed forces of all parties to their bases and barracks; and the holding of a referendum in Western Sahara before December 1980 under the joint supervision of the OAU and the United Nations. POLISARIO accepted the plan but maintained that no referendum held in Western Sahara would be genuine without the complete withdrawal of all Moroccan troops from the territory. Morocco opposed the plan and questioned the authority of the committee to draw up such a plan.

When Morocco saw that its support within the OAU was waning as a result of its uncompromising attitude, the Moroccan monarch made a surprise appearance at the 18th OAU Summit in Nairobi in June 1981. He announced to relieved, but sceptical African leaders his acceptance of what he called "controlled referendum whose modalities should give justice simultaneously to the objectives of the ad hoc committee ... and Morocco's conviction regarding the legitimacy of its rights."[39] No further debate took place on the issue. The summit simply converted the *Committee of Wisemen* into an Implementation Committee with Kenya as chairman and Guinea, Mali, Nigeria, Sierra Leone, Sudan, and Tanzania as members. The Implementation Committee was mandated to meet before the end of August 1981 to draw up the modalities for a cease-fire and a referendum with the help of the United Nations[40]

As soon as the Implementation Committee began its work, it became obvious that King Hassan's notion of a referendum was quite different from that of the OAU and the United Nations. Morocco would not allow the option of independence to be offered to the people of Western Sahara. The Moroccan monarch also refused to negotiate face to face with the representatives of POLISARIO at a meeting of the Implementation Committee in Nairobi from August 24 to 26, 1981. The Algerian leader was not prepared to negotiate on behalf of POLISARIO. As a result, the committee had to consult with each party individually.

At the end of the meeting, the Implementation Committee could do no more than issue a set of guidelines for the referendum. These guidelines made provision for a referendum on self-determination that would offer the people of Western Sahara the choice between independence and integration with Morocco. Eligible voters in the referendum, which would be organised by the Implementation Committee in collaboration with the United Nations would include Sahrawis on the Spanish census list of 1974 aged from 18 upwards and Sahrawis refugees in neighbouring countries documented by the United Nations. The guidelines called for the negotiation of a cease-fire by the parties under the auspices of the Implementation Committee and the installation of an impartial interim administration that would work in collaboration with the existing Moroccan administration. Also included in the plan was the deployment of an OAU/UN peace-keeping force to assist the interim administration, while all existing troops in the territory would be confined to their bases.[41] Subsequent meetings failed to overcome the impasse created by Morocco's refusal to negotiate with POLISARIO.

Frustrated by Morocco's intransigence and the apparent inability of the Implementation Committee to call Morocco to order, POLISARIO pursued its right to a seat in the OAU. Under pressure from the Pro-SADR majority group in the OAU, the Secretary-General finally sent a formal letter of eligibility in February 1982, as a result of which the SADR took its seat at the 38th ordinary session of the Council of Ministers in Addis Ababa on February 22, 1982.

The admission of the SADR paralysed much of the work of the OAU for the rest of the year and much of 1983. Throughout 1982, no OAU institution could hold any conclusive meeting. The 19th OAU Summit could not be held in Tripoli as scheduled. It was not until June 1983 that the summit was held in Addis Ababa. Then, it was only because the SADR had been persuaded by its supporters to withdraw temporarily from the meeting. The Implementation Committee made one last, fruitless attempt to bring the parties to the negotiating table in Addis Ababa in September 1983.

By the 20th summit of the OAU, which began in Addis Ababa on November 12, 1984, several members of the Implementation Committee had accorded SADR formal recognition and withdrawn from the Committee, thereby further swelling the number of countries that had accorded the SADR formal recognition. With no fewer than 31 member states according the SADR recognition, the SADR delegation took its seat at the summit as the 51st member of the organisation. Morocco immediately gave notice of its withdrawal from the organisation. Zaire was the only Member State, which, in sympathy with Morocco, suspended its membership. Zaire, however, has since rejoined the organisation.

The admission of the SADR undercut the OAU's mediatory efforts. It compromised the idea of a referendum on which the OAU's peace package hinged. At its 20th Summit, the OAU noted the report of the Implementation Committee, documenting its unsuccessful attempt to mediate in the conflict. The report, including the peace plan adopted by the OAU Assembly in 1983, was forwarded to the United Nations, to which the OAU, in effect, handed over the Morocco-Western Sahara conflict. Since then, the United Nations has assumed the position of the principal mediator, with the OAU playing only a supporting role.

The UN General Assembly subsequently endorsed the OAU

peace plan. There was, however, no immediate breakthrough in the efforts that were being made at the United Nations to effect a lasting solution to the conflict. It took another six years of sustained efforts by the UN Secretary-General, acting in close consultation with the various chairmen of the OAU, to formulate a set of settlement proposals that were acceptable to the two parties in conflict. The set of proposals, together with an implementation plan drawn-up by the UN Secretary-General, were unanimously approved by the Security Council on June 27, 1990. This was followed on April 29, 1991, by the establishment of the UN Mission for the Referendum in Western Sahara (MINURSO) by the Security Council.[42] A budget of $200 million was approved by the UN General Assembly for MINURSO.

The referendum, originally scheduled for the early part of 1992, and expected to be jointly supervised by the OAU and the United Nations, was not held that year. The people of Western Sahara were to be offered three options: independence, integration with Morocco, or autonomy under Moroccan sovereignty. The OAU/UN peace plan was to be implemented over a period of 40 weeks, involving a total manpower of 2,895, comprising 900 international civilian personnel, 300 police personnel, and a military unit with a strength of 1,695 (including 550 military observers and an infantry of 700 men).[43] Despite the delay in organising the proposed referendum, which, as at 1999, is still on the drawing board, there is general optimism in OAU/UN circles that if the referendum is successfully held, it will provide the basis for a lasting solution to the conflict.

In the light of severe political difficulties which the Morocco-Western Sahara dispute posed for the OAU, its failure to effect a cease-fire (never mind a final resolution of the conflict) is not surprising. With its members deeply divided on the issue; with its institutions for a time paralysed by the resultant acrimony; and with a powerful member-state like Morocco determined not to compromise, the OAU was incapacitated to act decisively and forcefully.

The OAU's management of the conflict between Morocco and Western Sahara underscores several weaknesses of the organisation, including its inability to raise a peace-keeping force, its perennially inadequate financial resources, the absence of an effective mediatory organ and, hence, its over-reliance on conference diplomacy. The conflict also demonstrates the OAU's need for an organisational mechanism to impose and enforce sanctions against parties reluctant to negotiate. Unable to exercise any leverage over Morocco, the OAU had to return the conflict to the United Nations. The OAU appears to have been guided in the later period of its management of the conflict by the organisation's earlier experience in Chad. This is obvious from the emphasis placed on joint UN/OAU peace-keeping operations in Western Sahara.

Chad demonstrated OAU's ineffectiveness in raising the needed finances to service a peace-keeping operation. As at the time of writing (1999), the organisation is yet to put in place any concrete plan for servicing a peace-keeping operation. Thus, in order not to repeat its peace-keeping fiasco in Chad, the OAU is being attracted to the idea of a joint UN/OAU peace-keeping arrangement in Western Sahara. What form the proposed UN/OAU partnership would take is, however, yet to be properly articulated. It calls for a serious dialogue between OAU and UN officials for the idea to be properly concretised. The success of such a partnership will be a commendable step towards actualising former UN secretary general, Boutros Boutros-Ghali's dream of lightening the burden of peace-keeping for the UN through the delegation of responsibilities to regional organisations.[44]

Summary of OAU's Performance

A detailed comparative analysis of the conflict management performances of the OAU and OAS is the subject of chapter 7. Meanwhile, a few general remarks about the cases analysed above seem appropriate.

Taken as a whole, the OAU's conflict management record is one marked by elaborate efforts and minimal results. Political divisions within the OAU, the determination of one or more parties to a conflict to press for a zero-sum outcome, and the impact of powerful external forces on African conflicts, are among the factors that have hampered, and sometimes effectively prevented, the peaceful settlement of disputes among OAU member states. Even so, the OAU might well have enjoyed more success had it not suffered both from structural defects and from a gross inability to exploit the full range of available techniques of conflict management.

Structurally, the OAU's insufficient institutional machinery for organising and maintaining a peace-keeping or monitoring force has limited the organisation's ability to sustain cease-fire agreements, while its lack of an effective permanent mediatory organ has greatly undermined its ability to sustain protracted negotiations between parties in conflict. These basic defects have led the OAU to rely excessively on ad hoc committees of heads of state and foreign ministers as its primary mediatory organs. These ad hoc committees have proved inadequate to the task of intensive and continuous mediation. Inevitably, given their already over-burdened workloads, the members of these committees have had neither the time nor the energy to commit themselves to long-term mediation. Furthermore, the frequent changes in the membership and leadership of these bodies has undermined continuity and done little to enhance the institutional memory of OAU conflict management efforts. And, as the Morocco-Western Sahara and Uganda-Tanzania conflicts painfully illustrated, political considerations have at times dominated the proceedings of the ad hoc committees, preventing any attempt at probing the fundamental issues behind the conflicts in order to find their appropriate and enduring solution.

As for its application of different conflict management techniques, the OAU has relied greatly on conference diplomacy and summit resolutions. These techniques undoubtedly have their value, especially in reaffirming pertinent principles and in adding the legal and moral weight of the organisation in support of the negotiating process. They also serve the purpose of abating conflicts through appeals to the parties and securing the commitment of the parties to pacific settlements. But conference diplomacy and summit resolutions, without question, have their limitations; they should not constitute the primary or the only organisational efforts at conflict management. They need to be followed-up with sustained negotiations between adversaries in order to resolve the fundamental issues underlying conflicts. This is the area where other conflict management techniques such as problem solving can be extremely useful to third-party mediators. The OAU's lack of resources is also a significant handicap, one that has played a major role in the organisation's failure to monitor cease-fires and organise peace-keeping operations. Inadequate resource support has indeed been an endemic problem since the organisation's formation. One scholar has accurately described the OAU as "materially undernourished" and noted that it has "little prospect of a new influx of resources."[45]

With the majority of its members labouring under the yoke of the debt burden, the OAU needs to devise a form of collaboration with the United Nations in its conflict management efforts; especially in the area of peace-keeping. However, if the organisation is to benefit fully from such collaboration, it must first create the necessary machinery for servicing peace-keeping operations.

Notes

OAU documents consulted in this study are essentially primary documents located at OAU Headquarters in Addis Ababa, Ethiopia. They are available in various files, while some are in bound copies. The documents relating to the meetings and decisions of the Council of Ministers are the CM Series while those relating to the meetings and decisions of the Assembly of Heads of State and Government are the AHG series.

1. M.A. Odesanya, "Reflections on the Pacific Settlement of Inter-state Disputes," in T.O. Elias ed., *Papers of the Third Annual conference of Nigerian Society of International Law* (Benin City: Ethiope, 1972), p. 49.
2. Patricia Berko Wild, "The Organisation of African Unity and the Algerian-Moroccan Border Conflict: A Study of New Machinery for Peace-keeping and for the Peaceful Settlement of Disputes Among African States," *International Organisation* 20 (Winter 1966), pp. 19-20.

3. *Ibid.*, p. 21; and I. William Zartman, "The Sahara-Bridge or Barrier?" *International Conciliation*, no. 541 (January 1963), pp. 15-18.
4. Algerian Ministry of National Orientation, *The Bamako Communiqué* (Algiers: Ministry of Information, March 1964).
5. *OAU Annual Review*, no. 1 (Addis Ababa, May 1964), p. 38.
6. Patricia Berko Wild, *op. cit.*, p. 33.
7. Sven Hamrell, ed., *Refugee Problems in Africa* (Uppsala: Scandinavian Institute of African Studies, 1967), pp. 14-15.
8. *CM/71*, Council of Ministers, Fifth Ordinary Session, Accra, October 10, 1965, *Report of the Administrative Secretary-General*.
9. CM/267/Rev.1, February 1969.
10. *AHG/Decl. 1 (iii)*, Addis Ababa, November 1966.
11. The report about the settlement was made to the Fourth Ordinary Session of the Assembly of Heads of State and Government in Kinshasa in 1967.
12. *African Research Bulletin* (March 15, 1989) p. 9167.
13. Notes 1 and 2 are in the Introduction to this study.
14. *AHG/Dec. 108 (XIV)*, Libreville, Gabon, July 1977.
15. *AHG/180 (XXVII)*, Report by His Excellency, El Hadj Omar Bongo, President of the Republic of Gabon, Chairman of the OAU Ad Hoc Committee on Chad/Libya Dispute, Abuja, Nigeria, June 1991.
16. *Keesing's Contemporary Archives*, February 1, 1980, p. 30065.
17. During various discussions with key participants in the peace-keeping efforts, including the Force Commander Colonel (later Major General) Magoro, between 1980 and 1985, this author was told of the harassment with which the force had to cope, including a campaign mounted by the French and Habre to discredit the force.
18. *Keesing's Contemporary Archives*, February 1, 1980, p. 30067.

19. *Ibid.*, October 30, 1981, p. 31160.
20. *AHG/Res.102-103 (XVIII)*, Nairobi, Kenya, June 1981.
21. $192 million was the revised estimate of the OAU Secretary-General; made upon the advice of a UN technical team. The first estimate was $162,897,500. See *AHG/109 (XIX)*, Report of the Secretary-General on Chad, Addis Ababa, Ethiopia, June 6-11, 1983, Part 1.
22. C.O.C. Amate, *Inside the OAU: Pan-Africanism in Practice* (New York: St. Martin's Press, 1986), p. 183.
23. *Ibid.*
24. OAU's request letter sent to the UN Security Council by Current Chairman, President Arap Moi of Kenya, circulated as Security Council document S/15011, April 29, 1982.
25. Security Council *Resolution 504*, April 30, 1982.
26. *West Africa* (weekly Magazine), December 21-28, 1981, p. 3096.
27. *AHG/ST/CTTEE/TCHAD/Res. 1 (III)*, Nairobi, Kenya, February 1982.
28. Europa, *Africa South of the Sahara*, 21st edition (London: Europa, 1992), p. 725.
29. Relevant resolutions include General Assembly Resolutions 2229 (XXI) in 1966, 2354 (XXII) in 1967 and 2428 (XXIII) in 1968.
30. Amate, *op. cit.*, pp. 330-331.
31. *Ibid*, p. 338.
32. *AHG/Res. 81 (XIII)*, Port Louis, Mauritius, July 1976.
33. AHG/Res.92 (XV), Khartoum, Sudan, July 1978.
34. AHG/Res.114 (XVI), Monrovia, Liberia, July 1979.
35. UN Document A/AC.109/621, August 8, 1980, p.6.
36. AHG/AHC/WS/Res.1 (III), Monrovia, Liberia, December 1979.

37. AHG/Dec.118 (XVIII), Freetown, Sierra Leone, July 1980.

38. AHG/103 (XVII)B, Report of the Fifth Session of the Ad hoc Committee of Heads of State on Western Sahara, Freetown, Sierra Leone, September 9-11, 1980.

39. African Contemporary Record, 14, 1981-1982, p. A69.

40. AHG/Res.103 (XVIII), Nairobi, Kenya, August 1981.

41. AHG/IMO/C/WS/Decl. (1), Nairobi, Kenya, August 1981.

42. UN Security Council Resolution 690, April 29, 1981.

43. Copy of the Statement by His Excellency, Yoweri Kaguta Museveni, President of the Republic of Uganda and Current Chairman of the OAU, at its 27th Summit, Abuja, Nigeria (unpublished), p. 7.

44. Boutros Boutros-Ghali, *An Agenda for Peace* (New York: United Nations, 1992), p. 37.

45. William J. Foltz, "The Organisation of African Unity and the Resolution of Africa's Conflicts," in Francis Deng and I. William Zartman, eds., *Conflict Resolution in Africa* (Washington, D.C.: Brookings Institution, 1991), p. 347.

Chapter 6

The Practice of Conflict Management by the OAS

FIVE inter-state conflicts in which the OAS has sought to play a conflict management role are examined here. Taken together, the five conflicts – Costa Rica-Nicaragua, Haiti-Dominican Republic, United States-Cuba, El Salvador-Honduras, and Argentina-United Kingdom – illustrate both the range of conflict types that have beset the region since the end of World War II and the kinds of responses that those conflicts have elicited from the OAS. Given the sheer number of cases that could be examined (Appendix 1 lists 34), choosing just five is no easy task, and some important conflicts have inevitably been excluded. Most notable of these exclusions is, perhaps, the civil strife that erupted in the Dominican Republic in 1965 and 1966 which led to unilateral U.S. intervention. That intervention was roundly condemned by nearly every member of the organisation for violating the non-intervention clauses of the OAS Charter. Ironically, however. OAS involvement in the conflict, though ostensibly intended to end the U.S. unilateral action, merely provided multilateral cover for the U.S. intervention. Ninety percent of the OAS Inter-American Peace Force was made up of U.S. forces, and the United States took care of almost 100 percent of the logistical needs of the operation. As such, the conflict clearly exposed the inability of the OAS to act except in those cases where U.S. interests are served.

This case, though undoubtedly important, is not examined here because the same lesson – how a regional hegemon can often effectively dictate the policies of a regional organisation – can be learned from other cases that also illustrate other facets and dimension of conflict management in the Americas. For instance, the United State-Cuba and Argentina-United Kingdom conflicts, which are examined here, teach the same lesson while also showing how the extra-regional concerns of the United States influence its activities within the American hemisphere.

Particular attention is paid in the following case studies to show not only the way that the OAS structure worked in practice, but also which conflict management processes were actually employed by the organisation. Like the OAU's CMCA, the OAS's Inter-American Peace Committee (IAPC) would seem to have been the organ best suited to the third stage within the conflict management circle, namely, the resolution of conflicts. However, as we shall see (and again much like the fate of the CMCA), the IAPC fell into relative disuse after its formalisation by the OAS, and thus most conflicts were handled by other organs.

The Costa Rica-Nicaragua Conflict (1948-1956)

Background

The conflict between Costa Rica and Nicaragua, which continued intermittently between 1948 and 1956, is traceable to the events that led to the rise of Jose Figueres to power in Costa Rica. Figueres took power through a successful revolt in 1948 against the government of Teodoro Picardo Michalski, which had maintained friendly relations with Anastacio Somoza's government in Nicaragua. Figueres's revolt was carried out with the help of the Organisation of the Caribbean Legion, which was committed to overthrowing all the autocratic governments in the region, including those of Nicaragua, Honduras, Venezuela, and the Dominican Republic. In 1947, Figueres had concluded an agreement (known as the Pact of the Caribbean) with various exile-groups, in which he pledged that if they helped him and his followers to come to power, he would use Costa Rica as a base for liberating all the countries in the region under dictatorships.[1]

This association with the pro-democracy movement, and hence the anti-government forces in Nicaragua, automatically put Figueres in the position of an opponent rather than a friend of that government. Thus, the conflict between Costa Rica and Nicaragua was first and foremost a system conflict, embedded in the ideological differences between the leaders of the two countries. The conflict later took on elements of a refugee conflict when the leaders of both countries encouraged anti-government activities by dissidents from each other's country.

The conflict actually erupted in December 1948, when about 1,000 Costa Rican exiles invaded the country from Nicaragua, where they had been carrying out activities against Figueres' government with the full support and encouragement of the Nicaragua regime. Although some of the invaders were captured, others continued with the struggle until the OAS intervened. For its part, the Figueres government was sponsoring the Caribbean Legion in its attempt to overthrow the government of Nicaragua. The hostilities between the two countries continued intermittently with major flare-ups in 1954 and 1955, before the dispute was finally resolved.

The OAS Response

The conflict was brought to the attention of the OAS on December 11, 1948, by the Costa Rican ambassador, who charged that the government of Nicaragua had violated Article 6 of the Rio Treaty by supporting an invasion of his country. He requested the convocation of the Permanent Council of the OAS, to act as the Provisional Organ of Consultation in accordance with Article 12 of the Rio Treaty. The council met on December 12 and adjourned for two days to study the problem. When it reconvened, it heard both the charges levied by Costa Rica against Nicaragua and the latter's rebuttal and counter-charges against the governments of Costa Rica and Guatemala of harbouring bands of revolutionaries – the Caribbean Legion – whose activities were a threat to peace in the region. Constituting itself as the Provisional Organ of Consultation, the Council established a five-member committee, known as the Committee of Information, to investigate the complaints. The Committee included representatives of Brazil, Colombia, Mexico, Peru (which did not participate), and the United States. It was chaired by Luis Quintanilla of Mexico.

The Committee began its assignment on December 17, 1948, with a three-day visit to Costa Rica. The members held consultations with Costa Rican officials, interrogated prisoners and persons allegedly associated with the Caribbean Legion, and visited the province where most of the hostilities had taken place. After two days of consultations and interviews in Managua with

Nicaraguan officials and others, the committee returned to Washington and presented its report to the Provisional Organ of Consultation on December 24, 1948.

The Committee's report blamed both sides for similar reasons. Although it found no evidence of direct involvement by Nicaraguan forces in the invasion, it noted that the Nicaragua government had failed to prevent revolutionary activities by Costa Rican exiles against their home government. At the same time, the report noted that the Costa Rican government was giving material and moral help to the Caribbean Legion. The Provisional Organ of Consultation approved the text of the resolution submitted by the Committee that called on both governments to immediately abstain from any hostile act against each other. It declared that the Nicaraguan government should have taken adequate measures to prevent the development in Nicaragua of revolutionary activities against the government of Costa Rica. It also called upon the Costa Rican government to take measures to rid its territories of groups organised on a military basis and conspiring against the security of Nicaragua and other republics.[2]

The Council created a five-member Inter-American Commission of Military Experts to oversee the implementation of these resolutions. The Commission completed its assignment by the end of January 1949, and reported that the two governments had complied with the Council's resolution. Other measures taken by the Council included a suggestion to the two governments to set up a mixed commission to deal with border control problems, and the drafting of a "Pact of Amity", in which both governments pledged to abide by their obligations to refrain from intervention in each other's affairs. Although the two government signed the "Pact of Amity", there is no record that the proposed border commission was set up.

While the OAS's timely action helped to defuse what was an explosive situation, it did not resolve the fundamental issue of how to effectively control the dissident exiles; so the underlying animosity between the two countries remained. Because no mechanism was set up for the effective monitoring of the activities of dissidents along the common border, it was only a matter of time before hostilities erupted anew.

On July 25, 1954, Costa Rican border forces, responding to another raid by Costa Rican exiles operating from Nicaragua, shot at and hit a Nicaraguan plane. The incident provoked an immediate military mobilisation by Nicaragua and a counter-mobilisation by Costa Rica. Only timely action by the United States in sending planes to Costa Rica prevented a bloody war. With no attempt being made to follow up the U.S action with serious mediation to address the fundamental issues behind the conflict, hostilities flared up yet again the following year.

When the OAS Permanent Council received complaint of a new invasion that occurred on January 11, 1955, involving about 500 men, it again constituted itself into a Provisional Organ of Consultation, and set up another Investigation Committee made up of representatives of Brazil, Ecuador, Mexico, Paraguay, and the United States and chaired by Ambassador Quintanilla. This time, in addition to calling for OAS action against Nicaragua, Costa Rica requested military assistance from the OAS Council for Military Aid, to help put a permanent halt to this perennial violation of its territory.

After a thorough investigation, in which it flew observation missions over the affected border, the Committee confirmed the attack and Nicaragua's complicity in it. It also confirmed air activities along the common border and noted Costa Rica's lack of aircraft with which to respond. On the basis of these findings, the council adopted a resolution under which the United States expedited the sale of four P-51 combat planes to Costa Rica. The sale of the planes gave Costa Rica control over its air space and a military advantage over its opponent. The council also arranged for the Investigation Committee to prepare, in consultation with the governments of the two countries, a plane for the effective surveillance of the common border. The two parties agreed to the establishment of a security zone on both sides of the border, and an air corridor to be patrolled by aircraft of the committee. The OAS efforts at resolving the conflict were concluded on January 9, 1956, with the two countries signing a new bilateral agreement on political exiles.

By getting the parties to agree on the issue of the conduct of political exiles and the establishment of a security corridor, the

OAS laid the foundation for meaningful negotiations to take place to achieve a lasting settlement of the very sensitive issue of political exiles. Thus, the OAS succeeded largely in not just abating, but resolving some vital aspects of the conflict.

The only aspect of the conflict that was not effectively resolved was the ideological one. Ideological or system differences are frequently aggravated when states fail to subscribe to the principle of tolerance. In encouraging such tolerance, the norms of behaviour established by inter-governmental organisations can be very helpful. Unfortunately, the OAS is ambivalent on the subject. On the one hand, the OAS Charter specifically enjoins its members not to interfere in one another's internal affairs. Yet, on the other hand, the Charter opens an avenue for such interference by stating a preference for representative democracy. Although it could be said that Figueres' support for the Caribbean Legion was in tune with the OAS preference for representative democracy, the position of the OAS in this case upheld non-interference rather than Article 3(d) of the Charter which committed member-states to representative democracy.

The Haiti-Dominican Republic Conflict (1949-1963)

Background

The conflict between Haiti and the Dominican Republic sprang from a complex mixture of system and refugee factors, which were exacerbated by the countries' peculiar geography. The two republics share the island of Hispaniola. Thus, they are the only two sovereign states with a contiguous landmass among the island states in the Caribbean Sea. They are thus ill-placed to escape the consequence of any disturbance in the other's territory.

The catalyst for the conflict was the decision in February 1949 by the Dominican Republic to grant asylum to the former Haitian army officer, Colonel Astrel Roland, who, with the help of some Dominican officers, had sought to overthrow the esteemed regime in Haiti. Ignoring Haiti's request not to grant Roland refuge, the Dominican government also took no action to check his propagandist activities against the Haitian regime. It may be noted that the Haitian government similarly tolerated the activities of Dominican dissidents opposed to the Trujillo regime. In late 1949 and 1950, the dispute escalated as the two governments traded accusations of invasion plans and subversive activities. The last major outbreak of intermittent hostilities between the two countries occurred in 1963, when on April 27, escapees from the tyrannical government of Francois Duvalier in Haiti sought asylum in the Embassy of the Dominican Republic. At the same time, Haiti was alleged to have been supporting opponents of the democratic Bosch regime in the Dominican Republic. By August 5, 1963, a force of Haitian exiles invaded their country from the Dominican Republic and occupied areas along the border.

The OAS Response

On February 16, 1949, Haiti invoked the Rio Treaty, and for the first time brought before the OAS Council its complaint about the subversive activities of Colonel Roland, noting specifically his radio campaign against the Haitian government. The reply of the Dominican Republic was that Roland was stating his private opinions over a private radio station. The Dominican Republic also noted that Haiti had called for the convocation of an Organ of Consultation without any effort at bilateral negotiations, and challenged the applicability of the Rio Treaty to the conflict. After listening to the representatives of the two countries, the council recessed for one week to consider the matter. A number of Council members doubted the applicability of the Rio Treaty to the Haitian complaint, many of them thought that the issue could be best handled by the IAPC. When it reconvened on February 23, the Council therefore refused to convoke the Organ of Consultation, and merely expressed the hope for good and friendly relations between the two countries.[3]

Reacting to the Council's preference for an IAPC response to the problem, Haiti decided to bring the complaint before the committee. The IAPC met to consider the matter on March 24, 1949, and decided to mandate a three-member delegation comprising Argentina, Mexico, and the United States to mediate the conflict rather than adopt the investigative approach. As a result of this mediation, a joint declaration was signed by representatives of both parties and the members of the committee on June 9, 1949, under which the two governments entered into a commitment not to "tolerate in their respective territories the activities of any individuals, groups, or parties, national or foreign, that have as their object the disturbance of the domestic peace in either of the two neighbouring Republics or any other friendly nation."[4]

Despite this declaration, peace was short-lived, as both countries traded verbal hostilities. By December 1949, relations between the two countries had again deteriorated. Haiti accused the Dominican Republic of violating the joint declaration by supporting the subversive activities of Haitian exiles intent on carrying out assassination plots against Haitian officials, and charged that the Dominican government planned to use the resulting chaos as a cover to invade Haiti on the pretext of protecting Dominican nationals. On January 3, 1950, Haiti formally requested the OAS Council to convoke the Organ of Consultation under Articles 6 and 8 of the Rio Treaty to take action against the Dominican threat. For its part, the Dominican Republic, after rejecting the Haitian charges, requested the Council to also consider the subversion against it from Haiti, Guatemala, Cuba, and Venezuela.

After considering both complaints on January 6, the Council, acting as the Organ of Consultation, set up a five-member Investigation Committee that included representatives of Bolivia, Colombia, Ecuador, Uruguay, and the United States. The Committee was authorised to investigate the facts and their antecedents referred to in the submissions of the two countries. It was to appoint its own chairman and establish its own procedures. The expenses of members of the Committee (excluding their adviser) were to be paid by the Pan-American Union, which was then functioning as the OAS General Secretariat.

The Committee carried out its assignment between January 12 and March 13, 1950. It undertook extensive visits to the two countries, interviewing not only government officials but also political exiles and prisoners. The report of the Committee portrayed a web of plots and counter-plots, propaganda campaigns, illicit arms traffic, the organisation of revolutionary expeditions, and official complicity in a number of these activities.[5] The report substantiated the Haitian claims, and only substantiated the Dominican claim only with regard to Cuba and Guatemala. The Committee also noted the underlying tensions in the Caribbean, which it attributed to the lack of effective democracy in some of the countries and the excessive accumulation of arms by some governments.

On the basis of the Committee's report, the Council passed resolutions declaring the actions of the Dominican government in relation to Haiti, and those of Cuba and Guatemala in relation to the Dominican Republic, to be contrary to the principles of the Inter-American System. The three governments were asked to take steps to ensure that these principles would henceforth be observed. Other resolutions called for an OAS study of measures to stimulate the effective exercise of democracy and improve the rules governing the activities of political exiles. The Council decided to set up a Special Committee to oversee relations among the countries in the area and to observe and report on compliance with the decisions of the Organ of Consultation. The Special Committee's reports were to be made available to the governments of the OAS through the General Secretariat.

The Special Committee held several meetings with the parties to the conflicts between April 1950 and May 1951, and received reports from the governments involved. It produced three reports that noted that several governments had initiated measures that had helped to promote goodwill, and that relations among the countries of the Caribbean had improved. The committee also noted the re-establishment of diplomatic relations between Haiti and the Dominican Republic and the fact that the two countries had agreed to work out measures to regulate their political, economic, and social relations.

As in the Costa Rica-Nicaragua case, here the OAS succeeded in taking timely action to abate a crisis that could have resulted in a major conflagration, though the organisation was unable to deal with the underlying causes of tension. The decision to establish the Special Committee to assist in the process of developing friendly relations between the parties was a good innovation and suggests an awareness of the limitations of the Organ of Consultation in effectively responding to a protracted conflict.

However, the uneasy peace that followed the 1950 understanding did not endure for a long time. Relations between the two countries worsened again with the coming to power in 1962 of an elected democratic government in the Dominican Republic, following the assassination on May 31, 1961, of the dictator, Generalissimo Trujillo. The new government, headed by the self-styled "crusader for democracy," Juan Bosch, was the antithesis of Duvalier's tyrannical regime in Haiti. President Bosch had great personal animosity for the Haitian leader, who he compared to Hitler and characterised as a "demented crazed man" of the "type found in primitive societies."[6] Believing that Haiti would remain unstable as long as Duvalier ruled, Bosch saw it as his historic mission to eliminate the Duvalier dictatorship and "liberate" the Haitian people.

Duvalier's oppressive rule intensified the refugee problem between the two countries. Fresh hostilities broke out in 1963 with the occupation of the Dominican Embassy by Haitian police searching for Haitians who had taken refuge there. The Dominican president responded to this incident with a 24-hour ultimatum that Haiti withdraw its police from the embassy, pay reparations, give assurance of improved future conduct, and issue a safe conduct pass to the refugees in the embassy. Failure by Haiti to carry out the above demands was to be met with an appropriate Dominican response. The ultimatum was followed by the deployment of Dominican troops to the border between the two countries. The matter was referred to the OAS Council when Haiti refused to accede to the Dominican demands.

The OAS Council met on April 28, 1963, to hear the usual charges and counter-charges from the two countries. The Dominican representative demanded OAS action to halt the violation of its embassy, put an end to terrorist tactics against Haitians seeking asylum, and denounce the assassination plot against President Bosch. The Haitian representative, denying the Dominican charges, complained that the Dominican government was interfering in the internal affairs of Haiti and was planning to invade his country. Acting provisionally as the Organ of Consultation, the Council appointed a five-member Investigating Committee to look into the conflict.

The Committee, comprising representative of Bolivia, Chile, Colombia, Ecuador and El Salvador, carried out its investigations in the two countries between April 30 and May 8, 1963. It secured, after much persuasion, an undertaking from the Haitian government that it would fully guarantee the safety of all diplomatic embassies and the refugees in them, and would permit all refugees who wished to leave Haiti to do so. The Committee was subsequently issued a new, less restrictive mandate to carry out an "on-the-spot study of the situation existing between Haiti and the Dominican Republic and to offer the parties its services for the purpose of finding a prompt solution to the conflict."[7] This new mandate enabled the Committee to examine all the issues involved in the conflict.

The Committee's report portrayed the embedded tensions between the two countries as arising largely from the systemic differences between the two regimes and their inability or unwillingness to control the activities of political exiles. The best solution to the conflict, the Committee noted, would be for both governments to comply with existing agreements requiring all hemispheric governments to control the activities of resident exiles. It noted, however, that the Bosch government had turned down Haiti's offer to enter into a new agreement to regulate the activities of exiles on the basis of "strict reciprocity."[8]

The Council adopted the Committee's recommendation on July 16, 1963, and appealed to both governments to refrain from the use of force and to submit their disputes to pacific settlement procedures. The Council urged Haiti to grant safe-conduct to refugees still in diplomatic asylum in Port-au-Prince and to respect human rights. It also expressed concern over the presence in Haiti of members and associates of the Trujillo family. The Council urged both governments to observe the various inter-American agreements on territorial asylum and control of the illegal activities of exiles.[9]

The Council had barely finished its work when it was faced

with a fresh complaint of an attempted invasion of Haiti by Dominican-backed Haitian exiles on August 5, 1963. The alleged invasion was said to have been led by Haitian General Leon Cantave, who later fled to the Dominican Republic.

The Investigating Committee was authorised by the Council to continue its work, but its efforts at mediation were complicated by the breakdown of diplomatic relations since the last controversy. After shuttling between the two capitals to explore avenues for reconciliation without success, the Committee drafted two-resolutions for the parties to release simultaneously in their respective capitals. These resolutions committed the parties to the application of appropriate international agreements with respect to the specific problems of exiles and asylum-seekers, and to accept the supervision of their shared frontier by the OAS for as long as conditions required. The Dominican Republic, although initially agreeable to the declaration, backed out at the last minute. In the end, the Committee simply noted in its report that its previous recommendations were an adequate basis for the solution of the outstanding problems between the two countries, and expressed the hope that the two parties would resort to bilateral negotiations to that end. The dispute was thus not fully resolved. When it did disappear, it did so because of the military overthrow on September 25, 1963, of Bosch's democratic government after which the Dominican Republic ceased to be a rallying ground for Haitian pro-democracy elements.

The responses of the OAS to this conflict demonstrate the limitations of the organisation's investigative method. Investigation, as its name denotes, seeks to examine the authenticity of accusations and counter-accusations by the parties in conflict and to discover which side is at fault. Within an organisational context, investigation thus provides merely the basis for a judgement or pronouncement on a given conflict. It does not provide sufficient room for intensive negotiation between the parties in conflict for the purpose of harmonising their interests. Between March and June 1949, the OAS through the IAPC attempted some conciliatory methods, which produced a joint commitment by the two parties to check the hostile activities of political exiles in their respective countries. However, the OAS did not sustain this effort on the long run to ensure that concrete measures were actually taken to translate this commitment into action. Apparently, it felt that the two parties can continue with the peace process unaided, and this turned out to be wrong. The Council's decision to set up a Special Committee for the continuous exploration of avenues for resolving the conflict indicates an awareness of the need for a mechanism for sustaining negotiations over a protracted period. It is ironic that the final recommendation of the Investigating Committee expressed the hope that the two parties would resort to bilateral negotiations to effect a lasting solution to the conflict, even though the OAS had failed to provide the necessary organ to facilitate the process of such negotiations.

The United States-Cuba Conflict (1959-1964)

Background

The conflict between the United States of America and Cuba contains elements of all the conflict types identified earlier in this study. Although essentially a system/ideological conflict, it also had elements of resource, territorial, hegemonic, and refugee conflicts. Furthermore, while the eruption of this conflict is traceable to Fidel Castro's rise to power in Cuba, it cannot be fully explained without recognising U.S. interests in the region, which were threatened by the change of government in Havana. Before Castro came to power, Cuba's export-oriented, sugar-based economy was extremely dependent on the United States, which accounted for two-thirds of Cuba's exports and three-quarters of its imports. There was also considerable U.S. investment in Cuba. It is estimated that U.S. investment in Cuba as of 1959 – in sugar, mining, utilities, banking and manufacturing – exceeded that in any other Latin American country except Venezuela.[10]

These economic interests have combined with strategic concerns to ensure enduring U.S. interest in Cuban affairs. Located in the heart of the "American Mediterranean", Cuba has been a strategic jewel coveted by the major powers since the opening up of the American hemisphere. U.S. intervention in 1898 led to the defeat of Spain and a temporary take-over of the island by the United States. In granting Cuba independence in 1902, the United States retained the right to intervene in the territory under what came to be known as the Platt Amendment. The United States has also operated a naval base at Guantanamo since 1903, under the terms of a treaty that guarantees the U.S. right to operate the base indefinitely. Castro, who has refused to recognise these treaty rights and has never redeemed the monthly checks paid to the Cuban government by the United States, has used the Guantanamo base as an effective ideological rallying point. Besides, U.S. support had also helped to ensure the success of a military coup in Cuba in 1933 led by Fulgencio Batista Zalvidar, who remained the dominant figure in Cuban politics until his overthrow in 1959.

Castro's seizure of power threatened U.S. interests in several ways. First, the new regime in Cuba came to subscribe to communist ideology, which the United States was committed to containing globally. Although there is no evidence of Soviet involvement with Castro's movement up to the time of Batista's overthrow, subsequent events created a growing estrangement between the United States and Cuba and forged closer ties between Cuba and the Soviet Union.[11] Second, Castro's regime threatened U.S. hegemony not only in the Caribbean, but in the hemisphere as a whole. The situation was aggravated by the declared commitment of the Cuban revolutionaries to export their revolution to the other countries of the hemisphere. Third, Castro opposed the continuing existence of Guantanamo base. And fourth, the Castro regime threatened to nationalise privately owned enterprises, thereby endangering U.S. investments. Many key players in the Batista regime and other opponents of the revolution fled to the United States, where they found fertile ground for planning and executing subversive activities against the new Cuban government.

The mistrust with which the regime was greeted by the United States was soon reinforced by the wave of nationalisation of private enterprises, which began in November 1959 and carried on into 1960 with the nationalisation of petroleum refineries in July. By October 29, the United States withdrew its ambassador in Havana. In January 1961, the United State broke off diplomatic relations with Cuba.

The simmering antagonism boiled over into open hostilities on April 17, 1961, when Cuban exiles, with the help of the United States, attempted an invasion of Cuba, landing at the Bay of Pigs on the south coast of the country. Although U.S. servicemen did not appear to have participated in the invasion, which was swiftly crushed by government forces, there was strong evidence of the Central Intelligence Agency's involvement. As far back as March 17, 1960, President Dwight Eisenhower, had authorised the CIA to organise the training of Cuba exiles for the future invasion of Cuba. However, the plan was carried out during the administration of John F. Kennedy, who allowed it to proceed "provided that U.S. forces were not used."[12]

The Bay of Pigs incident, together with the economic blockade the United States imposed on Cuba in response to the nationalisation of U.S. enterprises, drove Castro's Cuba closer to the Soviet Union. On July 9, 1960, Prime Minister Nikita Khruschev made an official commitment to defend Cuba. As he put it figuratively "in case of need, Soviet artillerymen can support the Cuban people with their rocket fire should aggressive forces in the Pentagon dare to start intervention against Cuba."[13] This was to become a reality in October 1962 when U.S. intelligence reported a Soviet missile build-up in Cuba. Apparently scared by the prospect of another U.S.– instigated invasion of their country, the Castro regime had fully embraced Soviet military protection. The level and nature of the Soviet military build-up in Cuba posed a grave danger to the security of the United States, which was therefore determined to see that Soviet missiles and nuclear warheads were withdrawn from the island. As the superpowers squared up to each other, a global catastrophe seemed very possible.

The OAS Response

Before the conflict between Cuba and the United States erupted into open hostilities, the OAS had already taken measures in response to various charges of subversion and support of dissidents levied against the new regime in Cuba. The first accusation came from Panama in April 1959, and centred on an attempted invasion of that country from bases in Cuba. With Cuban co-operation and assurances that steps would be taken to prevent future expeditions being mounted from its territory, the OAS Council was content to take measures through its Investigating Committee to effect aerial and naval patrol of the Caribbean waters adjacent to the coast of Panama. The Council also adopted a resolution that enjoined "any government that has reason to believe that there are persons in zones under its jurisdiction" participating in activities against the territorial integrity of Panama "to use all means to prevent such activities."[14]

Further accusations of Cuban support of dissidents were made by Nicaragua and the Dominican Republic. The Council's investigation, however, did not, find any connection between the Cuban government and the dissidents operating against Nicaragua, although some arms used by them were traced to Cuban sources. Most of the arms captured from the dissidents were, however, said to have been bought from the black market in Costa Rica, the country accused of giving the greatest support to the dissidents. The Council failed to act on the charges from the Dominican Republic, apparently because council members viewed Trujillo's dictatorial regime with the same distaste that many Dominicans felt.

Nonetheless, in the light of the numerous charges and counter-charges of support for dissidents, the 5th Meeting of Consultation of Ministers of Foreign Affairs in 1959 instructed the IAPC to carry out a study of international tensions in the Caribbean. In its report entitled "Tensions in the Caribbean Area," the IAPC pointed out that in addition to the activities of exiles resulting from the refusal of certain governments to permit the exercise of representative democracy, a new factor had been introduced through the danger of extra-continental subversion by the Soviet Union and the denial of human rights by dictators who disguised their disregard for human liberty under the banners of democracy and welfare.[15]

The first serious consideration of the Cuban-U.S rift by the OAS took place in San Jose, Costa Rica, in August 1960, during the 7th Meeting of Consultation of Ministers convened to consider the problem of communist intervention in Cuba. Seeking to reach a consensus at the meeting, the United States played down its system conflict with Cuba by emphasising not the communist threat in Cuba itself, but rather the danger Cuba's foreign policy posed for hemispheric security. The U.S. proposal concentrated on intervention by the Sino-Soviet bloc, the threat of armed attack by those forces, and the export of communism from Cuba to other countries in the hemisphere. It called for the "vigorous condemnation" of intervention in the hemisphere and the expression of "grave concern" over Cuba's encouragement of such intervention.[16]

Cuba responded by portraying itself as a victim of U.S. unilateral intervention. Presenting the Cuba case, Foreign Minister Raul Roa stated that the gravest danger to the hemisphere was not the hypothetical extra-continental threat, but the actual threat to continental security and peace resulting from repeated acts of harassment, reprisal, and aggression by the U.S. government toward Cuba. He alleged that Washington's aim was to destroy the progressive and anti-capitalist Cuban revolution and return Cuba to the "political and diplomatic orbit" of the United States. The United States, said Roa, wanted to use the present meeting "to establish, by guile, calumny and falsehood the basis for a unilateral or collective aggression" against Cuba. He noted that Cuba's acceptance of Khruschev's declaration should be understood as the direct result of U.S. actions toward Cuba, especially, since the OAS had failed to offer the slightest criticism against "the aggressions Cuba has suffered."[17]

Most participants in the conference sought to bridge the gap between Cuba and the United States and encourage the return of Cuba to the inter-American system. There was general sympathy for Cuba among most Latin American countries at the conference; even the ultra-right governments, against whom Cuba's revolutionary exports were directed, did not offer an outright condemnation of Cuba. These countries stressed the principle of non-intervention and interpreted it widely to mean: non-intervention by the Soviet Union in hemispheric affairs, non-intervention by Cuba in Latin American affairs, and non-intervention by the United States in Cuban affairs. As one commentator has noted, there was practically no support for the United States position that Cuban domestic policy per se represented a potential threat to the peace of the hemisphere. As a result, the meeting chose to adopt a resolution of a general nature that condemned the intervention or the threat of intervention by an extra-continental power in the affairs of the American republics. It declared that the acceptance of extra-continental intervention by an American state endangers American solidarity and security, and that the inter-American system is incompatible with any form of totalitarianism. Finally, it reaffirmed the principle of non-intervention by any American state in the internal or external affairs of other American states, and reiterated that each state has the right to develop its cultural, political and economic life freely and naturally.

There is no record that the Bay of Pigs fiasco was brought before OAS. Apparently, the Castro regime was satisfied that the attempted invasion had been effectively crushed and had served to underscore the Cuban claim that it was an innocent victim of U.S. aggression. Even so, it is perhaps significant that the OAS did not register any condemnation of the attempted invasion in defence of its principle of non-intervention. Of course, the organisation could hardly have changed U.S. policy; but it could have at least noted its concern at the actions of the regional hegemon. Castro's decision to carry his case to the UN instead of the OAS saved the latter the embarrassment of formally taking a stand on the US action.

The Bay of Pigs incident propelled Castro's Cuba further along its revolutionary path and pushed the country, irretrievably into the Soviet camp; so much so that, on December 2, 1961, Castro proclaimed that he was a Marxist–Leninist and would remain so until his death. The Castro government was also emboldened by the initial success of its support for revolutionary groups in Latin America, a development that caused great alarm in Washington.

When the 8th meeting of Foreign Ministers was convened on January 22, 1962, in Punta del Este, Uruguay, the OAS found itself divided on how to deal with the situation in Cuba. The United States wanted a collective diplomatic and economic boycott of Cuba, and the establishment of an OAS mechanism to combat "Cuban subversion". Although the United States found greater support than before among Latin American countries; a few member-states remained sympathetic with the Castro regime. After a hard bargaining, the meeting declared that adherence to the doctrines of Marxism-Leninism was incompatible with the inter-American system and voted to exclude the Castro regime from participation in the OAS. The meeting also voted to suspend arms trade with Cuba. Six member-states – Argentina, Bolivia, Brazil, Chile, Ecuador, and Mexico – abstained from voting on the clause suspending Cuba from participation in the OAS. Finally, the meeting set up a "Special Consultative Committee" on security matters to advise member-states on problems of communist aggression and subversion.[20]

When the missile crisis erupted in October 1962, the possibility of a nuclear confrontation between the Soviet Union and United States turned the conflict into a global concern. Efforts to resolve the conflict were made at different fora. Attempts made at the United Nations were impeded by the differences between the two superpowers, although the Secretary-General, U Thant, was able to play a modest role as a mediator. The non-aligned nations also played their part, sending emissaries to Washington and Moscow to appeal to Kennedy and Khruschev to exercise restraint and enter into peaceful negotiations to settle the dispute amicably.[21]

OAS action on the missile issue served the purpose of providing a collective base for what was essentially unilateral U.S. negotiation with the Soviet Union. In his October 22 radio and television speech, President Kennedy had called for the dismantling of the missiles and indicated that the United States would establish a strict quarantine against the introduction of any offensive military weapons into Cuba. When the OAS Council met on October 23, 1962, acting as the Organ of Consultation under the Rio Treaty, it adopted a resolution calling for "the immediate dismantling and withdrawal from Cuba of all missiles and other weapons with any offensive capability." It recommended that member-states "take all measures, individually and collectively, including the use of armed force, which they may deem necessary, to ensure that the Government of Cuba cannot continue to receive from the Sino-Soviet powers military material and related supplies which may threaten the peace and security of the continent and to prevent the missiles in Cuba with offensive capability from ever becoming an active threat to the peace and security of the continent."[22] The Council also expressed the hope that the UN Security Council would dispatch UN observers to Cuba at the earliest possible moment. This resolution helped to strengthen the U.S. resolve to confront the Soviet Union on the missile issue. As a further demonstration of solidarity, some OAS members, including Argentina, the Dominican Republic, and Venezuela, sent token forces when the United States acted to blockade Cuba.

This show of OAS solidarity was followed by bilateral negotiations between Soviet and U.S. officials, including exchanges of notes between their heads of state. The issue was finally resolved on October 31, 1962, when the Soviet Union agreed to withdraw its missiles in exchange for a pledge from the United States that it would not invade Cuba. Thus, the missile crisis was settled on the basis of a compromise that satisfied U.S. security needs while allowing the Soviets to claim that, given the U.S. pledge, there was no further need for the missiles in Cuba.

Subsequent OAS actions were more or less a continuation of sanctions in response to charges of Cuban support for revolutionary elements operating in a number of Latin American countries. Thus, at the 9th Meeting of Foreign Ministers in Washington from July 21 to 26, 1964, the OAS extended its sanctions against Cuba to include an end to diplomatic relations and the suspension of sea communications and trade in all items except foodstuffs, medicines, and medical equipment. The OAS Council was authorised to rescind the sanctions by a two-thirds vote at such time as the government of Cuba had ceased to constitute a threat to the peace and security of the continent.

In its management of the conflict between Cuba and the United States, the OAS never addressed the fundamental issues. The organisation's response throughout was coloured by the U.S. cold war world-view. At the urging of the United States, the OAS virtually abandoned the non-interference commitment embodied in its charter in favour of coercive responses to dissuade Castro's Cuba from the ideological path it had chosen. No attempt was made by the organisation to seek an understanding of the concerns and fears of both Cuba and the United States in order to find a way of harmonising their interests, however difficult this might have been, and redressing the legitimate grievances on both sides. The OAS sanctions were used not as an adjunct to, but as a substitute for, serious negotiations between the hostile parties. This focus on coercive responses succeeded in suppressing the fundamental issues involved in the conflict, but it did nothing to resolve them. The problem the OAS faced in the U.S.-Cuba conflict touches the issue of the apparent helplessness of an inter-governmental organisation vis-à-vis a very powerful and over-bearing member. Admittedly, the OAS cannot impose effective coercive sanction on the U.S. but it can bring a moral force to bear on the latter and take a stand against its excesses as far as the issue of non-interference in the internal affairs of member-states is concerned. Equally, the OAS should be able to take a stand on the sensitive issues of nationalisation of foreign investments and the activities of political exiles and set up rules to guide its members on these issues.

The Honduras-El Salvador Conflict (1969-1986)

Background

The outbreak of full-scale war between El Salvador and Honduras in July 1969 was the culmination of tensions that had built up for many years over competing territorial claims and disagreements over each country's treatment of the nationals of the other. Honduras and El Salvador had contested a number of *bolsones territoriales* (pockets of territories) along their common border, as well as ownership of the island of Meanguera strategically located in the Gulf of Fonseca.[23] The lingering antagonism between the two countries was aggravated by the migration of large numbers of land-starved Salvadorans into Honduras as settlers. Resenting both this influx and the commercial superiority of the Salvadorans, who were flooding their country with Salvadoran industrial goods, the Hondurans acted to restrict Salvadoran access to land and jobs. In 1963, a law was passed prohibiting companies from hiring more than 10 percent of their workforce from among foreign nationals. In 1968, a decree was promulgated that prevented Salvadorans from gaining title to Honduran land.[24] In addition, the "illegal Salvadoran settlers" in Honduras, estimated to number about 300,000, faced constant harassment and deportation to the Salvadoran side of the common border.

The smouldering mutual resentment found expression on June 15, 1969, when a number of Hondurans were manhandled during the World Cup elimination match between the soccer teams of the two countries, played in San Salvador. In response to an inflammatory newspaper report, Hondurans back home attacked Salvadoran settlers. Tens of thousands of Salvadorans had to flee Honduras to escape what the Inter-American Commission on Human Rights later described as "unrestrained violence" and "excesses of brutality". Inundated by the flood of refugees pouring in from Honduras, and faced with mounting domestic pressure to act forcefully, El Salvador on June 26, 1969, broke diplomatic relations with Honduras. By early July, border incidents were reported. On July 14, Salvadoran forces invaded Honduras, claiming to be protecting Salvadorans resident there. The ensuing war, which came to be known as "the soccer war", lasted for twelve days and cost about 2,000 lives.

The OAS Response

The initial OAS response was to give its backing to the initiative taken by the countries of Central America to mediate in the conflict. The foreign ministers of Costa Rica, Guatemala, and Nicaragua had on June 27, 1969, offered to mediate following the break in diplomatic relations between Honduras and El Salvador. At about the same time, the OAS Secretary-General requested the Inter-American Human Rights Commission to report on both the incident at the soccer match and the subsequent violence against Salvadorans resident in Honduras. With nobody expecting the dispute to escalate into war, the first special meeting of the Permanent Council on the conflict on July 4, 1969, merely expressed the hope that the mediation efforts would succeed. As of now, the Council saw no need to send an investigation or observation team. However, the settlement plan proposed by the

Central American foreign ministers failed to satisfy either side, and the Salvadoran government yielded to mounting domestic pressure for an invasion.

The Council met again, at Honduras' request, on the same day that Salvadoran troops crossed into Honduras. Acting provisionally as the Organ of Consultation in accordance with the Rio Treaty, the Council resolved to create a committee of seven members "to study on the spot the situation that has arisen between Honduras and El Salvador and the events that have caused it and to report to the Council."[25] It also called for an end to the hostilities and requested the OAS Secretary-General to keep the UN Security Council informed of its decisions.

The Council adopted another resolution on July 18, 1969, ordering the suspension of hostilities to be effective at 10.00 p.m. that night and calling on both sides to withdraw troops from each other's territory within 96 hours. It authorised the use of both military and civilian observers to ensure compliance with the cease-fire and troop withdrawal, and to monitor how both sides carried out their undertakings to respect the lives and property of each other's nationals residing in their respective territories.

The seven-member committee, made up of representatives from Argentina, Costa Rica, the Dominican Republic, Ecuador, Guatemala, Nicaragua, and the United States, succeeded in bringing the war to an end, but encountered difficulties in securing the withdrawal of Salvadoran troops to their pre-war positions. Before it would withdraw its troops, El Salvador insisted on receiving guarantees on the future treatment of its nationals in Honduras, including compensation for the property and personal injury of Salvadorans who had been forced to flee from the country. Only the threat of sanctions persuaded El Salvador to withdraw its troops.

This threat was made at a meeting of the Council on July 23, at which the Council arranged for the Meeting of Consultation of Foreign Ministers to convene on July 26 to consider the imposition of sanctions. Meanwhile, the Salvadorans were shown a draft resolution formally declaring El Salvador the aggressor and calling for the suspension of trade with the country in petroleum products, machinery, spare parts, coffee, sugar, and cotton.

Initially, the OAS had adopted the strategy of blaming both sides for the conflict, even though, in accordance with OAS convention, El Salvador could be said to be more at fault for disregarding pacific settlement and going to war. Furthermore, the invasion, which penetrated deep into Honduras, was not a proportionate response to the injury suffered, and the invasion routes betrayed little concern with protecting Salvadoran nationals. Faced with the threat of sanctions, and with the OAS Secretary-General working hard to break the deadlock, El Salvador agreed to a cease-fire.[26]

On July 29,1969, at the 13th Meeting of Consultation of Ministers of Foreign Affairs, an agreement was reached that provided for the withdrawal of troops and guaranteed the safety of the nationals of each state. Following an announcement from the Salvadoran foreign minister that his government had decided to withdraw its troops from Honduras, the meeting passed two separate sets of resolutions. The first set took note of the Salvadoran foreign minister's undertaking, ordered the withdrawal to be effected immediately, and instructed the seven-member committee to see to its implementation. The second aspect dealt with the important issue of the protection of each other's nationals resident in the two countries. It emphasised the point that to ensure peace and security, it is necessary to give adequate and effective protection to all citizens of El Salvador residing in Honduras and also to Hondurans residing in El Salvador, and noted that the governments of El Salvador and Honduras have formally bound themselves to provide ... guarantees of the lives, personal safety, and property of each other's nationals resident in their territory.[27] The foreign ministers also resolved that the seven-member Committee created by the Council should continue its work and take "all the measures necessary for seeing to the faithful and precise fulfilment" of the guarantees.[28]

The withdrawal of Salvadoran troops from Honduras and the exchange of prisoners were accomplished without any hitch under the supervision of OAS military observers. The issue of treatment of each other's nationals was more delicate. The main problem related to the internment by the Honduran authorities of about 11,000 Salvadorans for fear they might engage in acts of sabotage. Many of these detainees were confined in unsanitary and crowded conditions without adequate medical attention. To ensure that these detainees were adequately protected and cared for, the OAS Secretariat, with the help of Inter-American Human Rights Commission, took responsibility for ensuring that their conditions were ameliorated and for their later release from internment. The OAS also helped in effecting the release of some 231 Hondurans who were held in El Salvador without charges.

After stopping the fight and effecting the withdrawal of troops, exchange of prisoners, and release of detainees, the task of finding a solution to the differences between the two parties reverted back to the Central American countries. The five Central American foreign ministers held a two-day meeting in Managua on December 3 and 4, 1969, and recommended the establishment of a Bilateral Working Group (BWG) to find ways of bringing about a progressive and gradual solution of the outstanding issues in the conflict between Honduras and El Salvador. Under the plan, an OAS moderator was to preside over the deliberations of the representatives of the two parties. The person chosen as OAS moderator was Jose A. Mora, former Secretary-General of the OAS.

El Salvador and Honduras failed, however, to fully exploit this excellent opportunity to resolve their differences. They could not easily get over old animosities and suspicions. Rather than turn the BWG into a body of permanent session to deal with the main issues of contention between them, they only met at infrequent intervals, and then with what one observer described as "all the formality of the Congress of Vienna"– an agreed agenda, welcome addresses, and final acts.[29] Although they reached agreement over such issues as the restoration of postal, telegraphic, and telephone services, very little progress was made on the larger issues of frontier closure and territorial claims. A call by the Meeting of Consultation on October 27, 1969, on both parties to permit free transit of goods through their territories and to settle their boundary questions by negotiation had caused an outbreak of anti-OAS rioting in Honduras, with students threatening to use force to prevent the passage of Salvadoran vehicles and goods. The issue continued to be a sensitive one, and skirmishes repeatedly disturbed the peace in the less accessible frontier areas between the two countries.

These skirmishes led to an increase in the size of the small force of OAS military observers and an enhancement of their capabilities through the supply of light aircraft. The situation also led to a meeting in Costa Rica of the Central American foreign ministers from June 2 to 4, 1970, at which they approved a plan to establish a security zone in order "to prevent the occurrence of incidents" on the border between El Salvador and Honduras. The idea was "to re-establish peaceful conditions in the border region," thereby "permitting the resumption of normal activities by the inhabitants and the return to the region of nationals of the respective countries who have left it."[30] The plan, which was given OAS blessing on June 9, was guaranteed by Costa Rica, Guatemala and Nicaragua. It was to be carried out under the supervision of the OAS military observers. The foreign ministers made it clear, however, that the plan "shall have no effect whatsoever on the juridical question of the territorial claims of the parties in the border region."[31] Nonetheless, the measures helped to stabilise the situation along the border.

The OAS management of this conflict was effective in terms of stopping the war and arranging for troop withdrawal and the exchange of prisoners. The threat of sanctions was particularly useful in securing a cease-fire. The timely action taken by OAS to provide protection for the Salvadorans in Honduras also helped. It helped to prevent further incidents that could have complicated the OAS peace efforts. The OAS also played a significant part in focusing attention on the human rights aspects of the dispute. However, the OAS again exhibited an inability to sustain the process of negotiations over a protracted period during which the issues underlying the conflict might be explored and resolved.

The border conflict between the two countries and the issue of closure of the Pan-American Highway by Honduras were not resolved. Honduras made the opening of the highway contingent upon El Salvador's willingness to resolve the boundary disputes. The Central American foreign ministers failed to get negotiations resumed on the boundary issue at that material time. Perhaps, time was needed for tempers to cool down before any meaningful negotiation could take place to resolve the long-standing issue.

Apparently, the OAS lacked the capacity to service such a prolonged process of negotiation. It was thus much later in October 1980 that the parties were brought into direct negotiation through the efforts of Dr. Jose Luis Bustamente Y Riveiro, an eminent Peruvian Jurist. The result was the establishment of a mixed commission to deliberate on the boundary dispute, with the understanding that the matter would be referred to the ICJ if the parties were unable to reach an agreement after a specified time. In 1986, President Azcona of Honduras and his Salvadoran counterpart, Jose Napoleon Duarte, signed an agreement under which they decided to refer the dispute to the ICJ at the Hague. As at the time of this write-up, the ICJ was yet to make a final pronouncement on the boundary issue. It is however understood that much of the border had been delimited.

The Argentina-United Kingdom Conflict (1982-1989)

Background

The conflict between Argentina and the United Kingdom over the Falkland Islands (called the "Malvinas" by Argentina and in Latin America), which lie in the South Atlantic, off the coast of Argentina, was unusual for the OAS in the sense that it involved an extra-regional state as one of the belligerents. The conflict is essentially a territorial one with roots dating back to the European colonial struggles of the 18th century. In 1767, France ceded its rights to the islands to Spain, then the colonial ruler of Argentina. When Argentina became independent, it decided, as Spain's heir, to establish settlements on the Falklands, which hitherto had no permanent inhabitants.

Although it is difficult to say exactly when Argentina settlers first arrived on the islands, but by the 1820s the Argentine colony was flourishing as a result of a boom in the fishing and whaling industry. The United States was a major participant in that industry, with its ships venturing as far south as Tierra del Fuego and the Falklands. Despite warnings from the governor of the islands against fishing in Argentine waters, U.S whalers persisted in doing so. In 1828, the authorities in the Falklands seized two U.S. vessels, which they accused of violating Argentine sovereignty. The incident provoked a drastic response from the U.S President Andrew Jackson, who dispatched the warship *Lexington* to Buenos Aires to negotiate the release of the ships. Failing in that, the captain, acting on his own, sailed to the Falklands, overran the islands, took the authorities captive, and virtually evacuated almost all the other inhabitants to Montevideo in Uruguay. There is no record that these inhabitants returned to the islands after the settlement of the dispute.[32] Thus the British expedition that arrived on the island in 1833 found an almost entirely unpopulated territory. In 1833, the Falklands became a British Crown Colony. Argentina refused to accept the British take-over of the islands, over which it has since continued to claim sovereignty.

The area's economic and strategic importance, as well as each country's interest in securing the island's rich fishing rights have fuelled the intensity of the competition between Britain and Argentina for the Falklands. There was also a widespread speculation that hydrocarbons will be found in the area, while its strategic importance relates to the area's indispensability, especially, concerning the conflicting Anglo-Argentina claims in the Antarctica.[33]

Before the situation exploded into open war between the two countries in 1982, attempts had been made to settle the dispute through bilateral negotiations. Progress in these talks was very limited, however. While Argentina was pressing Britain to end its occupation of the islands and accept Argentine sovereignty over them, the British were busy consolidating their position in the territory. The decision by the Thatcher government to build extended runways at Port Stanley and establish a permanent British garrison there gave Argentina the impression that Britain was determined to stay on the islands indefinitely. The British government declared that it would only accept Argentina sovereignty over the islands, if the inhabitants of the islands were agreeable to the idea. Accusing Britain of endless prolongation of the bilateral negotiations, Argentina announced in 1982 that it would seek other means to resolve the conflict. On April 2, 1982, it invaded the islands, expelled the British governor, Sir Rex Hunt, and replaced him with a military governor. The war that ensued ended on June 14 with the defeat of Argentina and the re-establishment of the British administration over the islands.

The OAS Response

The OAS intervened in the conflict when, in response to the Argentina invasion of the islands, the British decided to send a task force to liberate the islands from Argentina military occupation. On April 13, the Permanent Council met and expressed concern over the deterioration of relations between the two countries and expressed "its fervent hope that a rapid, peaceful solution can be found to the disagreement between the two nations within the context of the rules of international law." It then offered" its friendly co-operation" in the efforts toward "a peaceful settlement of the dispute that will avert once and for all the danger of war."[34]

Following a request from Argentina dated April 19, 1982, the Council decided to convene as the Organ of Consultation under the Rio Treaty. The 20th Meeting of Consultation took place on April 28. It reaffirmed the primary aim of the Inter-American System, which is to preserve the peace of the American hemisphere, and rejected the intervention of extra-continental or continental armed forces in any nation of the hemisphere. According to the meeting; "Argentina's rights of sovereignty over the Malvinas (Falkland) island, as stated in some important resolutions passed by various international fora, including the Declaration of the Inter-American Juridical Committee on January 16, 1976, which states: 'That the Republic of Argentina has an undeniable right of sovereignty over the Malvinas Islands', must be born in mind." It then passed a resolution in which it:

- urged the government of the United Kingdom to cease the hostilities it is carrying on within the security region defined by Article 4 of the Inter-American Treaty of Reciprocal Assistance, and also to refrain from any act that may affect Inter-American peace and security.
- urged the government of Argentina likewise to refrain from

taking any action that may exacerbate the situation;

- urged the two countries to call a truce and resume negotiations aimed at a peaceful settlement of the conflict, "taking into account the rights of sovereignty of the Republic of Argentina over the Malvinas (Falkland) Islands and the interests of the islanders'; and
- expressed the willingness of the Organ of Consultation to lend support, through whatever means it considers advisable, to the new initiatives being advanced at the regional or world level, with the consent of the parties, which are directed toward the just and peaceful settlement of the problem.[35]

Various efforts, including those of the United States, to avert a military collision between Argentina and Britain were unsuccessful. Although President Reagan initially stressed the need for finding a peaceful settlement between the two countries he regarded as allies, his administration's even-handedness on the matter did not endure. Once the war began, it became clear that his country's NATO ally took precedence over his OAS commitment. This influenced his decision to impose a military trade embargo on Argentina, while helping the British with intelligence. The United States was not alone in imposing trade restrictions on Argentina. Most members of the European Economic Community (EEC) had already done so.[36]

When the Meeting of Consultation was again convened on May 29, 1982, it expressed concern that the U.S government had decided "to apply sanctions against the Argentina Republic and also agreed to give its support, including material support to the United Kingdom, which contravenes the spirit and letter of Resolution I." It deplored the "economic coercive measures against Argentina by the European Economic Community, with the exception of Ireland and Italy." It noted that "the purpose of the Inter-American Treaty of Reciprocal Assistance is to assure peace, through adequate means, to provide for effective reciprocal assistance to meet armed attacks against any American State, and in order to deal with threats of aggression against any of them."

It then passed a resolution (Resolution II) in which it:

- urged the U.S government to order the immediate lifting of the coercive measures applied against the Argentina Republic and refrain from providing material assistance to the United Kingdom, in observance of the principle of hemispheric solidarity recognised in the Inter-American Treaty of Reciprocal Assistance;
- urged the members of the European Economic Community, and other states that have taken them, to lift immediately the coercive economic or political measures taken against Argentina; and
- requested the signatories to the Rio Treaty to give the Argentine Republic the support that each judges appropriate to assist it in this serious situation, and to refrain from any act that might jeopardise that objective[37].

This resolution changed nothing. The United States did not withdraw its support for Britain, which also continued to enjoy the solidarity of majority of its European allies. There is no record of any substantial material help being given to Argentina by the other OAS member-states, which offered instead only moral support. Refusing to accept the OAS position, Britain maintained throughout that it was defending the Islanders' right to self-determination against its usurpation by Argentina. Suffering from the incompetence of its military leaders and cut off from all the major sources for replenishing its military might, Argentina could not sustain the war for long. On June 14, 1982, the Argentine forces surrendered, ending almost two and a half months of their occupation of the Falkland Islands.

The inability of the OAS to give material aid to Argentina or help devise a face-saving peace arrangement was a great blow to the credibility of the organisation. The OAS's failure was due in large part to the defection of the United States, which demonstrated the low status it accorded the OAS in its policy calculations, especially when its European ties were balanced against the notion of hemispheric solidarity. The Argentina-United Kingdom conflict also plainly illustrated the dependence of the

OAS on U.S. political and material support; without which support, the organisation was reduced to issuing pious resolutions of no practical import.

Despite its military defeat, Argentina has not given up its claim to the Islands. For its part, Britain has enhanced its military presence to deter a possible future Argentina bid to retake the Islands. For some time after the war, the Argentine government refused to declare a formal cessation of hostilities until Britain agreed to negotiations on sovereignty. But Britain has maintained that the issue of sovereignty is non-negotiable. As a result, subsequent talks between the two countries have failed to resolve the conflict. The United Nation's repeated calls on the two countries to enter into negotiations to resolve the problem have failed to produce any results because of the fundamental disagreement on this issue of sovereignty. In a new constitution prepared after the war, Britain granted the islanders the right to self-determination. The Peronist victory in Argentina in May 1989 has led to some improvements in the relations between the two countries. Serious negotiations between the two countries took place in October 1989, as a result of which they agreed on the formal cessation of hostilities and the re-establishment of diplomatic relations at the consular level. Further negotiations in February 1990, ended with the announcement that full diplomatic relations were to be re-established, while Britain would end its naval protection zone around the island. Although the two countries have gone a long way in normalising their relations, the issue of Argentina's claim of sovereignty over the islands remained unresolved as at the time of this write-up (1999).

Summary of OAS's Performance

Taken together, the above case studies indicate that although the OAS, on several occasions, has been able to abate conflicts, it has been largely unsuccessful in resolving them. The provision of the Rio Treaty that enables the Permanent Council to meet provisionally as the Organ of Consultation has enabled the organisation to take timely action to prevent the escalation of disputes into major conflagrations. The fact that most of its interventions in regional conflicts have been conducted under the provision of the Rio Treaty, which is more suited to coercive enforcement than to the art of conflict resolution (being a mutual assistance treaty against threat), has led the OAS to rely heavily on ad hoc Investigating Committees. Typically, once an accusation of aggressive intent was made, the Permanent Council, acting as the Organ of Consultation, would set up an Investigating Committee to determine the facts of the case. Based on the Committee's report, the Council would make its own judgement.

However, the institutional gap left by this more or less legalistic approach – a gap that grew larger with the demise in 1985 of the IAPC – has contributed to the inability of the OAS to mediate conflict over a protracted period. This limitation has inspired several attempts to seek solutions to regional conflicts outside the OAS. A good example is the work of the *Contadora Group* made up of the foreign ministers of Colombia, Mexico, Panama, and Venezuela, which between 1983 ad 1987 tried to further the cause of pacific settlement in Central America. The main impact of the *Contadora Group* was its encouragement of Central American inter-state dialogue and negotiation as a way of reducing tensions and laying solid foundations for an enduring atmosphere of peaceful co-existence and mutual respect.

The OAS has apparently recognised that a sustained process of negotiations is necessary to achieving lasting solutions to conflicts. Hence, in the Haiti-Dominican Republic conflict, the OAS established a "Special Committee" for the continuous exploration of possible avenues for the permanent solution of the conflict. Such ad hoc arrangements, though well intentioned, cannot however, be regarded as effective substitutes for a more reliable permanent institutional arrangement.

Given the complex nature of almost all the conflicts that have erupted in the hemisphere since World War II, it has been apparent that no one technique will work in every case. The OAS has used a combination of techniques to good effect in the management of some conflicts. For instance, the use of observer missions (as in the Haiti-Dominican Republic case), the threat or use of sanctions (as in the Honduras-El Salvador and Cuba- United States cases), and the use of the IAPC (as in the Haiti-Dominican Republic conflict), illustrate how the use of a variety of techniques has enabled the OAS to prevent the escalation of a number of conflicts. Yet, though these techniques have proved effective at the conflict control stage of the conflict management circle, they have not allowed the OAS to operate effectively at the conflict resolution stage.

The OAS's frequent use of the provisions of the Rio Treaty has underlined its neglect of the Pact of Bogota. Even those states that have ratified the pact have been reluctant to avail themselves of its provisions for the purpose of resolving their conflict. Because of its reliance on the Rio Treaty, the OAS has tended to employ coercive forms of response and thus has been able to take firm action in some of the conflicts involving clear cases of aggression or threats of aggression, especially those involving the smaller powers. The organisation has been very weak in dealing with cases involving the interests of major powers or protracted negotiations over complex economic and political relationships.

Another significant weakness of the OAS has been its failure to design an effective response to the many system conflicts such as Costa Rica-Nicaragua and US-Cuba conflicts that involve developmental issues. Those few attempts to address the economic problems of the region have been made outside the framework of the OAS, not least because the organisation's financial pillar, the United States, has preferred to deal with other member-states on a bilateral or sub-regional basis in economic matters.

Overall, the position of the United States has remained a mixed blessing for the OAS. While its wealth and power provide the organisation with most of its resources, the United States has frequently exploited its dominant position, more or less dictating the ideological stance of the OAS during the cold war and acting unilaterally whenever it has suited her. Not surprisingly, the Latin American countries have resented this U.S. dominance. Their resentment helps to explain the relative enthusiasm with which they have participated in the *Contadora Group* and the *Lima Group* (the latter, made up of Argentina, Brazil, Peru, and Uruguay, was involved in Central American and Caribbean conflicts), both of which have operated independently of the United States. The lack of enthusiasm among the Latin American member-states for the creation of an effective OAS peace-keeping mechanism can also be traced to their apprehension that, with its overwhelming influence on the OAS, the United States might employ an OAS peace-keeping force to assist or camouflage unilateral U.S intervention in the region. Memories of the 1965 events in the Dominican Republic cannot but help to sustain such suspicions.

The behaviour of the United States raises the question of whether international organisations are helpless to check the actions of powerful hegemons. Within the United Nations, the frequent use of the power of veto by one or the other of the superpowers rendered the world body more or less impotent to discipline the actions of the United States and the Soviet Union throughout the cold war era. However, there is no power of veto in the OAS. This leaves open the possibility that while the OAS cannot realistically expect to restrain U.S behaviour through threat or the use of force or sanctions, the organisation could bring its moral weight to bear on an erring hegemon through such means as a policy of non-co-operation, the censuring of [U.S.] actions, and the imposition of temporary diplomatic boycotts. Such measures would be unlikely to damage the hegemon materially, but they might help to temper its behaviour and encourage self-imposed restraint. Of course, for this to happen, the members of the OAS would first need to muster the collective courage to apply the needed checks.

Notes

The OAS official documents used in this study, (especially the OEA and OAS series), were procured from the OAS Secretariat/ Library at Washington, DC. They are usually in loose form, representing Permanent Council or Meeting of Consultation of Ministers of Foreign Affairs resolution/decisions, or reports of ad hoc committees. Many of the documents were got through various desk officers in the secretariat or photocopied from the library.

1. Harold D. Nelson, ed., *Costa Rica: A Country Study* (Washington DC. American University, 1983), p. 43.

2. David W. Wainhouse, *International Peace Observation* (Baltimore: Johns Hopkins Press, 1966), p. 110.
3. *Ibid.*, p. 116.
4. *Ibid.*, p. 117.
5. *Ibid.*, p. 121.
6. Juan Bosch, *The Unfinished Experiment: Democracy in the Dominican Republic* (New York: Praeger, 1965), pp. 183-185, quoted in Robert D. Tomasek, "The Haitian-Dominican Republic Controversy of 1963 and the Organisation of American States," *Orbis* 12 (Spring 1968), p. 304.
7. Jerome Slater, *The OAS and United States Policy* (Columbus; Ohio State University Press, 1967), p. 304.
8. *Ibid.*, p. 225.
9. *Ibid.*, p. 226.
10. Leslie Bethell, ed., *The Cambridge History of Latin America*, Vol. VII, 1930 to the Present (New York: Cambridge University Press, 1990), pp. 219, 468; and Thomas E. Skidmore and Peter E. Smith, *Modern Latin America*, 2nd edition (New York: Oxford University Press, 1984), p. 256.
11. Nikita Khrushchev's remarks in his memoirs regarding Soviet ignorance of Castro's movement and events surrounding the fall of the Batista regime, quoted in Nicola Miller, *Soviet Relations with Latin America, 1959-1987* (New York: Cambridge University Press, 1989), p. 58.
12. Bethell, *op. cit.*, p. 463.
13. Miller, *op. cit., Soviet Relations with Latin America*, p. 76, from *Pravda*, July 10, 1960.
14. Wainhouse, *op. cit.*, p. 142.
15. Krieg, *Peaceful Settlement of Disputes through the OAS*, pp. 42-44.
16. Slater, *op. cit.*, pp. 144-145.

17. *Ibid.*, p. 145.

18. *Ibid.*, p. 147.

19. *Ibid.*

20. *OEA/Ser, C/II.8*, Eighth Meeting of Consultation of Ministers of Foreign Affairs. Resolution VI, Final Act, Pan American Union, Washington, D.C., 1962.

21. Full details of the missile crisis are available in many other works and do not require elaboration here.

22. *OEA/Ser. G/V. C-d-1024 Rev.*, Pan-American Union Council of the OAS Acting Provisionally as Organ of Consultation, Council Series Washington, D.C., October 23, 1962, not published.

23. William H. Durham, *Security and Survival in Central America: Ecological Origin of the Soccer War* (Stanford: Stanford University Press, 1979).

24. Skidmore and Smith, *op. cit.*, p. 323.

25. *OAS/Ser. F/II 13. Doc. 3*, Resolution adopted by the Council at its Special Meeting on July 14, 1969.

26. Robert D. Tomasek, "The Organisation of American States and Dispute Settlement from 1948 to 1981- An Assessment," *Inter-American Review of Bibliography 39*, no. 4 (1989), p. 473.

27. *OAS Doc. 29* (English), July 30, 1969, Thirteenth Meeting of Consultation of Ministers of Foreign Affairs, Resolutions and Declaration Approved (As of July 30, 1969).

28. *Ibid.*

29. Krieg, *op. cit.*, p. 68.

30. *OAS/Ser. F/II. 13 Doc. 9[illegible]*, June 9, 1970, Annex titled "Informal Meeting of the Ministers of Foreign Affairs of Central America, San Jose, Costa Rica, June 2 through June 4, 1970."

31. *Ibid.*

32. Jeffrey D. Myhre, "Title to the Falklands-Malvinas under

International Law," *International Studies 12*, No. 1 (Spring 1983), pp. 25-36.

33. Argentina, Great Britain, and Chile have sovereignty claims that overlap on the Antarctica Peninsula. For more on the claims to Antarctica, see Christopher C. Joyner and Blair G. Ewing, Jr. "Antarctica and the Latin American States: The Interplay of Law, Geopolitics, and Environmental Priorities," *Georgetown International Environmental Law Review*, 4, issue 1 (Spring-Summer 1991), pp. 1-46. See also Jack Child, ed., *Regional Co-operation for Development and Peaceful Settlement of Disputes in Latin America* (New York: I.P.A. Publications, 1986), pp. 113-116.

34. OAS Permanent Council, *OEA/Ser. GCP/Res. 359*, April 13, 1982.

35. OAS, *OEA/Ser. F/II. 20*. Doc. 28/82 rev. 3, Meeting of Consultation of Ministers of Foreign Affairs, Resolution I, April 28, 1982.

36. The *Sunday Times of London*, "Insight Team", *War in the Falklands: The Full Story* (London: & New York: Harper & Row, 1982), p.117. For U.S. later efforts to resolve the conflict, see "Argentina Study: A.U.S. Peace Plan," *The New York Times*, April 29, 1982.

37. OAS, *OEA/Ser. F/II. 20. Doc. 80/82 rev. 20*, Resolution II, May 29, 1982.

Chapter 7

Comparative Assessment of the Performances of the OAU and OAS

BOTH the OAU and OAS designed conflict management machineries that are more elaborate than those possessed by most Inter-Governmental Organisations (IGOs). When it came to putting these machineries into practice, however, both organisations exhibited many of the same limitations suffered by other IGOs: a piecemeal approach, the resort to improvisation, and a tendency to progress no further than the abatement of conflicts. In comparing the performances of the OAU and OAS, this chapter assesses not only the records of the two organisations but also the reasons for their limited success. It is argued that part of the explanation lies in defects in the conflict management structures created, and part in the failure to exploit the potential of the machinery that was established. For reasons outlined in the introduction to this study, less attention is given here to the impact of political interests and circumstances on attempts at conflict management in Africa and the Americas in recent decades. This is not to downplay the very considerable influence that such politics has inevitably had; rather, it is to permit, within this relatively short space, a clearer understanding of the ways in which organisational machinery has, or has not functioned.

The following discussion is organised into five sections, the first four of which assess, in turn, how the two organisations utilised their conflict management machinery; their abilities to respond quickly to conflict situations; the conflict management techniques used; and the level of effectiveness at each of the three stages within the conflict management circle. The fifth and final section discusses how their effectiveness could be improved.

Utilisation of Conflict Management Machinery

In addition to establishing institutions of the kind traditionally used by regional IGOs and the United Nations for conflict management, both the OAU and OAS went a step further by setting up special organs for the management of conflict. The OAU created the CMCA; the OAS set up the IAPC (later called the IACPS). The decision to establish these organs suggests awareness, on the part of the two organisations, of the need for a mediatory organ as part of their mechanisms for managing conflicts. As this study has shown, however, the CMCA suffered from complete disuse, while the IAPC operated for only a limited period before encountering the same fate as its OAU counterpart did.

The delay in setting up the machinery of the CMCA, its legal character, and its rigid procedures all contributed to the reluctance of OAU member states to use the Commission. Five years elapsed between the CMCA's establishment at the inaugural meeting of the OAU and its reaching a fully operational level. When, finally, it was ready to begin work, all its members were legal experts. Although the CMCA had the authority to undertake such functions as mediation and conciliation, its composition suggested to member-states that the Commission would favour judicial procedures instead. Consequently, member-states did not use it.

With the facilities of the CMCA left unused, the OAU had to resort to improvisation in the management of conflicts at the level of serious negotiations. The organisation had to rely on ad hoc committees in its efforts to get parties in conflict to negotiate and resolve their differences amicably. The OAU was not very successful in this regard because these ad hoc committees, made up of heads of state and government or foreign ministers, proved incapable of sustaining negotiations over a protracted period. At best, they would try to take the heat out of a conflict, present their report to the OAU, and then lapse into relative inaction, waiting for another subcommittee to take over in the event of a fresh outbreak of hostilities between the parties.

The OAS fared better with the IAPC, at least for a while. The idea behind the IAPC predated the pacific settlement instrument drawn up by the OAS under the Pact of Bogota in 1948. As the organ already saddled with the peaceful settlement of disputes within the OAS, the IAPC was seen as the appropriate organ to implement the mediatory functions provided for in the Pact of Bogota. However, with the pact yet to be formally ratified (and it was indeed never ratified) by sufficient member-states to become fully operational, the IAPC had to function informally. As soon as it lost its operational flexibility – following the 1956 decision to statutorily incorporate the IAPC into the mainstream of the OAS conflict management system trammelled by the rigid processes embodied in the Pact of Bogota – none of the member states was prepared to use it any longer.

During its relatively short operational life, the IAPC performed a useful role. For instance, it enjoyed some success in mediating in the conflict between Haiti and the Dominican Republic in 1949. It is difficult to say however, whether or not the Committee would have succeeded in effecting a lasting settlement between the two countries had the OAS Council, opting to use the provisions of the Rio Treaty, not removed the conflict from the jurisdiction of the IAPC.

When the IAPC fell into disuse, the OAS, like the OAU, resorted to improvisation and ad hoc arrangements. The ad hoc committees created by the OAS for managing conflicts were frequently comprised of foreign ministers or ambassadors accredited to the organisation. And because they were usually given limited mandates; they were ill-suited for the task of sustaining negotiations over a protracted period.

In terms of their activities at the level of conflict prevention and conflict control and abatement, both organisations possess institutional mechanisms with the potential to play significant roles. The OAU has the Assembly of Heads of State and Government, the Council of Ministers, the Defence Commission, and the Secretariat; the OAS has the Meeting of Consultation of Ministers of Foreign Affairs, the Permanent Council, the Advisory Defence Committee, and the Secretariat. Unfortunately, however, some of these organs have not been brought into the mainstream of the conflict management efforts of their respective organisations.

In the case of the OAU, the Defence Commission has been

relatively marginalised as far as conflict management is concerned. It has not been able to effect any plan for the establishment of a peace-keeping mechanism – something, which, as this study has shown, is vital to the enhancement of the OAU's conflict management efforts. The Defence Commission was also not quite successful in its attempts to persuade the Council of Ministers and the Assembly to strengthen the Defence Unit at the Secretariat, which has consequently remained under-staffed and under-funded. It should be noted that even if such organisational restructuring were to occur, the OAU would still find it difficult, if not impossible, to mount effective peace-keeping operations in the face of the omnipresent poverty of military, financial, and logistic resources from which Africa suffers. Nonetheless, if the OAU is to make the most of its meagre resources, it must overcome its wilful neglect of those institutional improvements which it can accomplish with relative ease. The organisation's lack of any contingency plan for peace-keeping and its woeful performance as a peace-keeper in Chad in 1982 testify to the results of this neglect.

The OAS Advisory Defence Committee and the Defence Board have similarly suffered from relative marginalisation as far as conflict management efforts are concerned. Even though the OAS has been able to organise a number of peace-keeping operations – thanks to the initiative and resources of the United States and a few other members – the Advisory Defence Committee and the Defence Board have played little or no role in these operations. Instead of using these institutions to evolve a permanent peace-keeping arrangement, the OAS has relied on ad hoc improvisation made possible by the goodwill of a few of its members. The net result is that the OAS, like the OAU, still possesses no reliable mechanism for undertaking peace-keeping or enforcement actions.

A plausible explanation for the institutional gaps in the structure of the conflict management systems of the OAU and the OAS relates to their failure to see conflict management as a holistic or integrated system in which the activities of all the organs within each organisation are mutually reinforcing. Viewed from this perspective, it becomes clear that if any conflict management exercise is to be effective, all the organs must function effectively. The failure by the OAU and the OAS to conceive of conflict management in this holistic way has meant that some vital organs have failed to receive the necessary attention and resource support, thereby fatally weakening the overall success of their conflict management efforts.

Of course, political realities too can frustrate the effective management of conflicts. Even so, without the full range of functioning conflict management structures in place, even those conflicts that are not bedevilled by formidable political difficulties cannot be effectively managed. Moreover, the existence of institutional gaps denies the opportunity for a hostile political climate to be gradually improved through the containment of a conflict or the encouragement of sustained and meaningful negotiations. For instance, were an effective peace-keeping mechanism in place, it could be used to bring some respite in hostilities between inveterate enemies, thereby enhancing prospects for negotiations to begin. Altering the political climate so that negotiations can begin and continue should be part and parcel of an organisation's conflict management approach.

Speed of Response

This study has shown that not only the institutional manner but also the timing of responses to conflicts can be critical to the eventual success of an organisation's management efforts. While there is no general agreement among scholars or practitioners as to the proper timing of third-party responses to conflict, William Zartman's theory of a "mutual hurting stalemate" enjoys wide acceptance. Zartman's concept of "ripeness" is, however, only useful when disputes have already escalated into open warfare. Within an integrated conflict management system, in which conflict prevention is as important as conflict control, Kenneth Boulding's emphasis on "catching conflicts young" is perhaps more valuable than Zartman's theory.

The success of the timely actions by the OAS in averting the escalation of a number of conflicts underscores the importance of Boulding's approach. While the timely action by the OAS in the

Costa Rica-Nicaragua conflict, for instance, helped to prevent its escalation, the organisation's relatively tardy response in the case of the conflict between Honduras and El Salvador did nothing to prevent it developing into open warfare.

What facilitates the process of quick response by the OAS, is the provision in the Rio Treaty that enables the Permanent Council to constitute itself as the Provisional Organ of Consultation for the purpose of taking action on the conflicts brought before it. Since the members of the Council are in permanent residence at OAS headquarters, it is relatively easy to summon them to a meeting at a very short notice. It would be a different matter if the OAS had to wait until it was able to arrange the Meeting of Consultation of Foreign Ministers to deal with such conflicts. One of the major weaknesses of the Pact of Bogota is that there is no established procedure for invoking its instruments. Thus, even if the pact were to be fully ratified, with the demise of the IAPC, there is no institutional provision for setting its instruments into motion.

Unlike the OAS, the OAU has been relatively ineffective in nipping conflicts in the bud. The OAU has no instrument like the Rio Treaty, permitting a timely response to conflicts. The requirement that, at least, two-thirds of its members must consent before an extraordinary session of the Council of Ministers could be summoned, has often led to costly delays. The difficulty in bringing foreign ministers together to deal with crisis situations has inspired the suggestion by Sierra Leone and supported by some OAU members, that the organisation should create a Political Security Council, made up of fifteen members, with four from West Africa, three each from East, North and Central Africa, and two from the South. Each member is to serve for two years during which its ambassador to the OAU would be resident at OAU headquarters and thus available at very short notice to attend to emergencies.[1] It is not yet known if this proposal will be reflected in the on-going review of the OAU Charter. As of 1999, the OAU has gone no further than creating a Conflict Management Division within the Political Department of the Secretariat.[2]

Conflict Management Techniques Used and their Overall Effectiveness

As earlier indicated in this study, there are basic similarities and dissimilarities in the approaches of the OAU and OAS to conflict management. Apart from the basic similarities in their institutional provisions, the actual utilisation of these institutions by the two organisations differs in various degrees. Another important area of their dissimilarity to be addressed here, has to do with the level of emphasis placed on the various techniques of conflict management by the two organisations, as well as the level of success recorded by them. In discussing these similarities and dissimilarities, attention will be focused on the three stages of the earlier highlighted integrated conflict management model in the following order: conflict prevention/peace promotion, conflict control/abatement and conflict resolution.

At the level of ***conflict prevention/peace promotion,*** this study shows that although both organisations have prescribed various behavioural principles intended to promote a climate of peace within their respective regions, the OAU seems to have done more than the OAS in reinforcing those principles during the course of its conflict management activities. Of particular interest in this regard, are the measures taken by the OAU, to the effect that members should respect the boundaries they inherited at the time of independence. Although these measures have not entirely eliminated boundary disputes, they have helped to diminish demands for the redefinition of Africa's international boundaries imposed by the former colonial regimes. The OAS has no similar provision.

The OAU Convention on Refugees is another good example of the organisation's peace promotion efforts. Unlike the UN Convention on Refugees, which makes the proviso that states may deny asylum-seekers admission for "overriding reasons of national security," the OAU convention made it virtually obligatory for member states to grant asylum to persons in need. In effect, the OAU has entrenched the principle of obligatory acceptance of refugees as an inter-state norm in Africa, thereby ensuring that no state can be blamed simply for accepting refugees. The OAU also laid down that, in return for the protection they receive, African refugees are obliged to respect the laws of their host countries and to refrain from any action against their countries of origin. Although the OAU convention has not completely eliminated inter-state friction arising from the problem of refugees, it has helped to mitigate its explosive potential.

The OAS has not been able to respond to the same problem in any effective manner, apparently because key members – most notably, the United States – see refugees as instruments of intervention against other regimes in the hemisphere. With the United States having used refugees in blatant attempts to destabilise governments in such countries as Cuba (through U.S. support for the forces that landed at the Bay of Pigs) and Nicaragua (through U.S. support for the Contras), and with the OAS so dependent on U.S. resources, it would surely be a futile exercise for the OAS to enact principles supposed to guide the behaviour of refugees.

Another principle, which the OAU (though surely not all its member states) seems to have scrupulously maintained, is that of non-interference in the internal affairs of member states. Indeed, adherence to this principle has had an unintended adverse effect on the OAU's conflict management capabilities. It has prevented the organisation from intervening in internal conflicts even where such conflicts have come to pose a greater threat to the security of the continent than do conflicts between states. As a way of mitigating its debilitating effect on the organisation's conflict management efforts, the principle of non-interference is being given a new interpretation within the OAU Secretariat, according to which the principle is seen as proscribing *unilateral* intervention by individual states in the internal affairs of fellow African states, but not collective action as expressed through the OAU, especially, for humanitarian reasons. The main exponent of this new thinking is the former Secretary-General, Salim Ahmed Salim.

The OAS commitment to non-intervention – a rather dubious commitment in the light of the actions taken by the OAS at the urging of the United States in places like Dominican Republic in 1963, Grenada in 1983, Nicaragua in 1982-1986, Panama in 1989 and Haiti in 1993-1994 – is also being reviewed. Some sense of the nature of the "new thinking" that is evolving from the late eighties within the OAS can be gleaned from the efforts being made to harmonise the two seemingly contradictory charter provisions on non-intervention and "representative democracy." With OAS members giving increasing importance since the late eighties to the promotion of democracy and the protection of human rights throughout the hemisphere, the organisation has mandated the Inter-American Juridical Committee to study this and other issues of apparent contradiction in the Charter.

Like the OAU, the OAS is moving towards developing a more structured form of collective intervention, especially in the areas of governance. Toward this end, in 1990 the OAS established within its Secretariat, a Unit for Democratic Development.[3] Issues bordering on democratisation in Africa have been broached in recent speeches by African statesmen, especially during and since the 1991 Summit in Abuja Nigeria. The OAU member-states have indeed taken a position against military rule in Africa at the December 1999 meeting in Pretoria. However, despite its declared zero tolerance to military rule, the OAU is yet to contemplate an institution similar to the OAS Unit for Democratic Development.

Both the OAU and the OAS have done little to promote integrative activities in their respective regions as a way of building mutual confidence and trust between member-states. Although the OAS countries had an early start on the road toward regional integration, they are now lagging behind the countries of some other regions, notably Western Europe. The relative inter-state harmony West European countries now enjoy owes much to the level of integration that has been achieved there. The European experience underlines the need for the OAU and OAS to recognise regional integration as a key component in their conflict prevention and peace building machinery.

In terms of overall effectiveness in the area of conflict prevention/peace promotion, the OAU and the OAS have not accomplished much beyond the establishment of various behavioural principles to promote harmonious relationship within their respective regions. While the establishment of a behavioural code is very important to the promotion of a climate of peace, by itself, it is insufficient for that task and must be reinforced by practical measures designed to foster trust and mutual confidence among member-states. One of the key measures that needs to be taken is the promotion of socio-economic and political co-operation at both the bilateral and multilateral levels within a region. As we have seen, both the OAU and OAS are yet to make regional integration meaningful to ordinary citizens by facilitating professional, social and economic contacts among them.

In Africa, for instance of late, especially from 1990, the OAU seemed to have shown greater interest in issues of integration by encouraging inter-state co-operation at both the regional and sub-regional levels. To this end, the member-states signed the African Economic Treaty at the 1991 Abuja Summit and the African Union Constitutive Act at the July 2000 Lome Summit. However, because these integrative moves have been essentially on paper, the organisation's efforts are yet to have any impact in terms of mitigating the colonial-imposed mutual isolation of the nationals of neighbouring African countries. Undoubtedly, greater integration within the continent could have a positive impact on the problems associated with boundary disputes by gradually discouraging the manifestation of territorial exclusiveness on the part of African states, and by encouraging joint economic ventures among them.

The OAS has not also achieved much as far as integration is concerned. Excessive unilateralism in developmental efforts has tended to foster inter-state rivalries, which have undermined the promotion of mutual confidence and trust among the countries of the hemisphere. This has unfortunately created the impression among member-states, especially the Latin American countries, that the OAS is not sufficiently responsive to the developmental needs of its members. The U.S. inclination to deal with the countries of the American hemisphere in economic matters on a bilateral basis, rather than through the framework of the OAS, has also contributed to the increasing irrelevance of the OAS as far as developmental problems facing the countries of the region are concerned.

The OAU and the OAS could also help to mitigate the chronic problem of intra-state conflicts by insisting on, and even collectively enforcing through the use of non-military sanctions, respect for human rights and the observation of principles and practices that serve as the building blocks of true democracy, such as guarantees of minority rights and meaningful participation of all citizens in the affairs of their countries. Apparently, in adherence to the principle of non-intervention in the internal affairs of member-states, the OAU has failed to promote the observation of minimum standards in the conduct of public affairs by African leaders. The organisation's Charter on Human Rights has remained no more than a document which member-states and their leaders ignore at will.

Notwithstanding its principle of non-interference, the OAS has sought to promote the tenets of representative democracy within the American hemisphere. It has not done so in a consistent manner, however. Many examples can be found of OAS member-states fraternising with dictatorial anti-democratic regimes for the sake of narrow national interests, in blatant disregard of the provisions of the OAS Charter and of their pro-democratic commitments. It is to be hoped that the organisation's Unit for Democratic Development will help to bring about a more structured and consistent collective approach to the promotion of democracy in the region.

In the area of ***conflict control/abatement***, the OAU and OAS have employed a variety of the familiar techniques of conflict abatement, a number of which have proved effective, albeit to varying degrees. The use of conference diplomacy has been very pronounced in the management of conflicts by the two organisations, both of which have used it successfully as a de-escalating technique. In addition, the OAS has effectively used peace-monitoring and peace-keeping forces as well as power politics techniques – like the use of threat or actual imposition of sanctions, arms balancing and arms embargo – in the management of a number of conflicts. By contrast, while the OAU has recognised the need for peace-monitoring and peace-keeping forces, it has not been able to mobilise the resources necessary for such operations. It has also been incapable if not unwilling to use power politics techniques in the management of conflicts.

In terms of overall effectiveness, it is at the level of conflict control and abatement that both the OAU and the OAS have been relatively effective. The OAS in particular, through a combination of persuasive and coercive responses, has been able to arrange a number of cease-fires and has ensured some level of compliance through the deployment of monitoring forces. In cases such as Costa Rica-Nicaragua and Haiti-Dominican Republic conflicts, the OAS was able to prevent them from exploding into open conflagrations, even though it was unable to resolve the fundamental issues involved.

Of course, abatement efforts have not always succeeded. The OAS failed to contain the conflict between Argentina and the United Kingdom. The organisation was more or less ineffective in the Cuba-United States conflict (indeed, the imposition of sanctions on Cuba merely compounded the conflict). Moreover, the dispute between El Salvador and Honduras exploded into open warfare before the OAS could control it.

The OAU too has its limitations in the area of conflict control and abatement. Of the five case studies, it was only in the Rwanda-Burundi conflict, apart from the Algeria-Morocco one which was effectively resolved, that OAU's abatement efforts achieved some success. Although the OAU was able to arrange a number of cease-fires, as in the Chadian and Uganda-Tanzania conflicts, it lacked the resources to monitor them effectively. As a consequence, hostilities often soon resumed leaving the matters to be settled on the battlefield. The failure or inability of the OAU to exercise effective leverage over arms suppliers to African governments and rebels has also contributed substantially to the failure of the Organisation to take advantage of stalemates in African wars. Even after suffering serious military setbacks, parties to a conflict are often reluctant to enter meaningful negotiations because of their expectation that arms suppliers will soon re-equip them with the means to continue their fight.

At the level of ***conflict resolution*** in which serious mediation becomes necessary, the OAU through various ad hoc committees, has tried such techniques as the provision of good offices and conciliatory measures, but these have not been pursued with sufficient consistency and for sufficient time to have the desired effect. The OAS has performed more of investigation than actual mediation, the reasons being that most of its interventions have been carried out under the framework of the Rio Treaty, which is directed against external aggression. Essentially, therefore, the OAS has tended to adopt a judicial approach, seeking to determine which of the parties in conflict is at fault and then, if necessary, imposing sanctions on the guilty side.

Because of the minimal role that serious mediation has played in the conflict management activities of both organisations, most of the available techniques of conciliation have been employed only occasionally and ineffectively. For instance, problem solving – defined here as an attitudinal disposition toward resolving the fundamental issues involved in conflicts – has been largely neglected. Both organisations tend to perceive conflict management not as an integrated activity in which the full range of techniques must be employed, but as an ad hoc and piecemeal business. As a result, the will to manage conflicts to their logical and mutually acceptable conclusion by resolving the fundamental issues involved has been conspicuously absent.

Thus, in terms of overall effectiveness at the level of conflict resolution, not much has been achieved beyond abating conflict through, especially on the part of the OAS, establishing and maintaining cease-fires. Of course, establishing and maintaining cease-fire are certainly important elements of conflict management, but by themselves they do not constitute successful conflict management, at least, not in its integrated sense. Success can only be claimed when the underlying issues in a dispute have been effectively resolved to the mutual satisfaction of the parties. Sadly, this is where the OAU and OAS have shown themselves to be particularly weak.

In the case of the OAU, the Algeria-Morocco conflict is one of the few that could be said to have been effectively resolved. Most others were left unresolved, or lapsed into stalemate, or were eventually settled in combat. The record of the OAS is no better. It has achieved some success (as in Haiti-Dominican Republic conflict), but for the most part, the conflicts brought before it have been suppressed (as in the case of the conflict between Cuba and the U.S.), negotiated outside the OAS (such as El Salvador-Honduras conflict), decided on the battlefield (like the Falkland war), or, as it has usually been the case, not resolved. Even the Haiti-Dominican Republic conflict was not completely resolved until political circumstances changed with the overthrow of the Bosch government.

Optimising their Conflict Management Performance

At least some of the failures of the OAU and OAS as conflict managers can surely be attributed to the simple fact that many of the conflicts the organisations were faced with were not amenable to easy resolution. When at least one of the parties to a conflict perceives the struggle as a zero-sum contest, and is determined and equipped to fight on until victory is secured, there is little a third party can do to bring the adversaries to the negotiating table. Unless of course, it is prepared or that it has the capability to carry out a coercive intervention to suppress the unco-operative party. Thus, for instance, Nyerere's determination to see Amin ousted from power in Uganda left the OAU helpless to broker a settlement once the conflict had been allowed to escalate into open warfare. Equally, the persistence of a pattern of adversarial political relations can effectively prevent any chance of a conflict being effectively resolved. Hence, for example, the Haiti-Dominican Republic conflict was not resolved until the fall of Bosch permitted a fundamental shift in the pattern of relations between the two countries. Similarly, it will be difficult to resolve the U.S.–Cuba conflict with the deep-rooted ideological differences between successive American leaders and Fidel Castro unless there is a change of leadership in Cuba.

The conflict management records of both organisations should also be judged in the light of constraints placed upon each organisation by the realities of their members' political and economic situations. The OAU, for example, has found it exceedingly difficult to mount peace-keeping operations mainly because its member-states, many of them poverty-stricken and severely under-developed, lack the resources needed to equip and sustain such missions. The OAS does not suffer from a similar dearth of resources, mainly because of the support it receives from the rich and powerful United States. However, that very same circumstance – the presence of a dominant power within the ranks of the organisation's members – places a different kind of constraint on the OAS. Unless the United States gives its support, the OAS cannot undertake any activity that requires significant economic or political strength. By the same token, the OAS as a whole, is often unable to resist U.S attempts to direct the organisation's activities and dictate its policy. The asymmetry of power that shapes so much of the OAS's activity is not to be found in the OAU, but the OAU is by no means immune from the consequences of power struggles among its members (as the Morocco-Western Sahara conflict clearly illustrated).

However, while it is important to recognise that the conflict management performances of the OAU and OAS are often constrained by ***circumstantial limitations*** (adverse political conditions, determined belligerents, lack of resources, political divisions within the organisation itself, and so forth), it is no less important to acknowledge the self-imposed ***institutional limitations*** (gaps in conflict management machinery, short-sighted and inconsistent policies, uneven adherence to codes of behaviour, and so on), under which the two organisations labour. While the first set of limitations might be relatively difficult to deal with, the latter is not beyond the power of the OAU and OAS to effectively address and remedy.

To improve their performances, both organisations must first develop a more realistic perspective regarding conflict management. As this study has demonstrated, their approaches to conflict management have rather been incoherent and inconsistent. They need to perceive conflict management, not as an ad hoc and temporary business, but as an integrated process, comprising conflict prevention and peace promotion, conflict control and abatement, and conflict resolution; with one level of response not only leading to, but mutually reinforcing the other, until the conflict is resolved to the mutual satisfaction of the parties involved. In other words, there must be a predisposition to go beyond conflict abatement and get at the root of conflict.

To manage conflict in this comprehensive manner, the OAU and OAS need to act in four areas where they are at present deficient. First, they must build a tradition of strict adherence to collectively developed behavioural codes by their member-states through the subtle use of sanctions. They also need to reinforce these behavioural codes with confidence-building and integrative measures to encourage maximum human contact within their regions, thereby promoting mutual understanding and trust. Because many of the inter-state conflicts in Africa and the Americas are spill-over from intra-state conflicts, the OAU and OAS should seek to include in their behavioural codes principles that will help to promote democratisation and respect for human rights and fundamental freedoms.

A second important area of weakness relates to the lack of effective machinery for peace-keeping and monitoring exercises. The OAU is particularly deficient in this area. Of course, the failure of the OAU to evolve effective machinery for peace-keeping and monitoring is more as a result of the organisation's lack of resources than of a lack of awareness of the usefulness of peace-keeping. The issue of an "OAU Defence Force", which could provide the framework for peace-keeping and monitoring operations, has been on the organisation's agenda since the Monrovia Summit in July 1979 which approved in principle the idea of creating such a force. Subsequent studies on how to translate the idea into practical reality have produced an appreciation of the financial costs involved, and this has diminished the earlier enthusiasm of member-states.[4]

At the Dakar Summit in 1992, as part of his proposal for a new conflict management mechanism for the OAU, the Secretary-General made a strong plea for member-states to have specially trained troops within their national armies to handle peace-keeping and monitoring operations for the OAU when necessary; but the proposal failed to receive the approval of member-states.[5] It was not until the mid-nineties, when events in Africa demonstrated the increasing reluctance of the international community to be involved in African peace-keeping, that the OAU member-states realised that they could no longer afford to stand aloof. Although they believed that the maintenance of international peace and security remained the responsibility of the United Nations Security Council, it was obvious to them that the world body was no longer eager to bail out Africa from the continent's endemic crises and conflicts. They felt that "certain exceptional circumstances can, and do arise," which may warrant "the deployment of limited peace-keeping or observation missions by the OAU." They therefore agreed that Africa should now seriously endeavour to develop and enhance its capacity in the field of peace-keeping. Thus, belatedly in June 1995, the Council of Ministers requested the Secretary-General to convene a meeting of the Chiefs of Defence Staff of Member-States of the Central Organ to discuss technical issues relating to peace-keeping by the OAU.[6]

As at the time of this write-up, the OAU is yet to concretise the suggested plan for the establishment of a peace-keeping force. The first meeting of the Chiefs of Defence Staff, which met in Addis Ababa in June 1996, recommended the principle of stand-by arrangements and earmarked contingents on a voluntary basis. It also stressed the need for proper co-ordination of the peace-support activities of the OAU and sub-regional organisations, stating that the OAU should take advantage of existing arrangements within the sub-regions. While accepting the above recommendations in principle, the Chiefs of Defence Staff were further requested to look into the issues relating to the logistics, finance, training, doctrine, structure and operational planning needed for its peace-support operations. Although it is gratifying to note that however much the OAU tried to resist a peace-keeping role, events in Africa is gradually pushing the organisation into accepting the inevitability of some form of peace-keeping involvement in the continent, one only hopes that this will not be the proverbial case of dragging an unwilling horse to the river without being able to force it to drink the water. In other words, one hopes that this would not be a repeat of the experience of the earlier mentioned "OAU Defence Force", which was accepted in principle at the Monrovia Summit in July 1979, a project that is yet to materialise.

Perhaps the OAU needs to adopt a loose set-up based on sub-regional arrangements. This will lighten the logistic and financial burden that could again frighten it away from actualising its present plan. In this sense, the suggestion by the Chiefs of Defence Staff that the OAU should take advantage of the existing arrangements within the sub-regions is pertinent. Lacking the capability to mobilise forces for peace-keeping on a continental basis, the OAU should devise a decentralised system based on sub-regional mobilisation as and when required. To ensure that the sub-regional units are able to provide, at short notice, the required troops for peace-keeping operations in their respective areas, a programme of joint training and joint exercises at sub-regional levels should be worked out. Such a programme would surely enhance the cohesiveness and efficiency of peace-keeping forces. Until it is in a position to mobilise the necessary resources from within to service a peace-support operation, the OAU should work out some form of collaboration with the United Nations.

Although the OAS has been able to carry out peace-keeping and monitoring operations on a number of occasions, the organisation still lacks reliable organisational machinery able to mount peace-keeping missions as and when required. To date, the OAS has had to rely on the goodwill and initiative of its members, particularly the United States. The OAS organs under whose responsibility the organisation might have evolved a peace-keeping force – the Inter-American Defence Board and the Advisory Defence Committee – have been more or less precluded from playing any role in the organisation's peace-keeping efforts. Two factors in particular have worked against the effective utilisation of these organs for organising an effective OAS peace-keeping and monitoring force. First, there is the reluctance of the civil authorities, especially in Latin America, to allow the military to play any prominent role within the organisation. The second has to do with the fear among Latin American countries of the degree of influence that the United States would exercise over such a force. However, in anticipation of a possible change in the attitude of member-states, the Inter-American Defence Board has drawn up plans to take on a peace-keeping role.[7]

A third weakness shared by the OAU and OAS is their lack of an effective mediatory organ. The fates of the CMCA and IAPC have been discussed at some length in this study. The fact that both bodies suffered from disuse should not be taken as a sign of the irrelevance of mediatory organs to the conflict management efforts of inter-governmental organisations. It does show, however, the reluctance by nation-states to use organs of mediation that are constituted as judicial outfits or are bound to adhere to inflexible processes.

Both the OAU and the OAS need permanent mediatory organs comprised of highly influential and experienced individuals drawn from a variety of disciplines and professions who can devote the time needed to help facilitate and sustain serious negotiations between the parties in conflict. Such an organ should be allowed a generous measure of flexibility in its operations. To assist the mediatory organ, the OAU and OAS should maintain small research units within their respective secretariats to help in the rapid identification of areas of potential conflicts and conditions likely to generate conflicts, thereby enabling the organisations to take swift preventive action. The research units should also help to collect data relating to the issues involved in the conflicts being handled by the mediatory organ. In other words, the research unit should serve as a data bank for the storage and retrieval of information on the conflict management record of these organisations, allowing the mediatory organ to learn from and build on past experiences.

In 1992, two parallel developments seemed to have brightened OAU's prospects of creating such an organ. The first was the establishment of the Elder-Statesmen Council for Peace. This Council, which is an outgrowth of the African Leadership Forum (founded by General Olusegun Obasanjo of Nigeria), was composed of highly respected former heads of states and leaders, which then included Obasanjo himself, Mwalimu Julius Nyerere of Tanzania, and Kenneth Kaunda of Zambia. Although the Council decided at its inaugural meeting in Arusha, Tanzania, in March 1992 to operate on a non-official basis, it had the potential of being harmonised with the OAU's conflict management process and serving as the organisation's mediatory organ. The respect, which the Council members enjoyed, combined with the moral weight of the OAU, could exert a major influence on parties in conflict throughout Africa. The fact that the Council members were no longer in charge of their respective countries would have allowed them to devote the time needed for effective mediation. Unfortunately, the enthusiasm, which greeted its formation, was not sustained towards the actualisation of its objectives.

Second, the OAU Secretary-General, Salim Ahmed Salim, received approval in principle for his proposals for a new OAU Conflict Management Mechanism and the establishment of a Division for Conflict Management in the Political Department of the Secretariat.[8] While approving the proposals, the Assembly of Heads of State and Government requested the Secretary-General to undertake "an in-depth study of all aspects" relating to the proposed conflict management mechanism, "including institutional and operational details, as well as its financing." Member-states were requested to submit "their views, comments and proposals" on it to the Secretary-General.[9] The document on OAU Mechanism for Conflict Prevention, Management and Resolution, which evolved from the wide consultations carried out by the Secretary-General was approved at the Cairo Summit in July 1993. It saw the formal establishment of the proposed division on conflict management, and provided for an enhanced role in conflict prevention and resolution for the Secretary-General, who is to function under the supervision of the Bureau of the Assembly of Heads of State and Government. Under the arrangement, the Secretary-General could take personal initiative with full consultation with the chairman of the Bureau to put in place pre-emptive measures to prevent the outbreak or escalation of conflicts, or to actually help in revolving such conflicts, possibly, through the use of special envoys or eminent persons.

As a way of ensuring that the new conflict management outfit is given the necessary resource backing, a special fund to be known as "OAU Peace Fund" was established. The fund is to be serviced partly through allocation from the ordinary budget of the OAU and voluntary contributions from states, individuals and institutions within and outside Africa.

Whether or not the new institutional arrangement would meet the needs of the OAU's conflict management efforts would now depend essentially on the initiative of the Secretary-General who has been given a lot of responsibility under the new arrangement. It will also depend on the extent to which OAU member-states are prepared to shed their lukewarm attitude towards their financial responsibility to the organisation and the seriousness with which they take their obligations to the Peace Fund. The truth is that even the most ingenious, active and committed Secretary-General still needs the necessary resource support to actualise the goals of the organisation. Admittedly, the Secretary-General can mould the new Division of Conflict Management to serve a multi-functional purpose, including serving as a research cell to support the work of the earlier proposed mediatory organ. Besides, since the present arrangement gives the Secretary-General some flexibility as to how to raise his team of mediators, he could also draw on the expertise within the new division, or elsewhere, for the purpose of meeting the need for a mediatory organ identified in this study as necessary for the effective resolution of conflicts. However, all these fine measures can come to naught if the Secretary-General fails to get the needed resource support.

The fourth deficiency of the OAU and OAS is their neglect of the problem-solving approach to conflict management. As it has been noted earlier, this approach entails regarding every conflict as a problem to be solved to the mutual satisfaction of the parties involved. Problem solving calls for comprehensive analysis of the issues involved in a conflict and seeks to counter or avoid fixed positions and notions. As such, it provides the opportunity to address all the interests, fears, and concerns of the parties involved in a conflict.

Which technique or techniques should be used to resolve the issues underlying the conflict depends on each individual case. Flexibility is vital, and the choice of techniques should be left to the mediation team involved. Methods might include gradually conditioning the parties to abandon their adversarial views of one another with the use of problem-solving workshops or second-track or multi-track diplomacy; the give-and-take process of needs satisfaction; and the redressing of legitimate grievances. What is important is not the method used but rather the attainment of a mutually acceptable and lasting solution. The usefulness of the problem-solving approach lies in the fact that it helps to create a disposition toward addressing the fundamental issues involved in conflicts – that is, it provides the overall strategy that governs the basic attitude of the third-party conflict manager.

If the OAU and OAS were to adopt the problem-solving approach, they would be much more likely to manage conflicts to their logical conclusion. This is not to say that they should at the same time abandon judicial and power-politics approaches. Each approach has its place within the conflict management process, and conflict managers should recognise where each of the various techniques is applicable, as well as their complementarity. For instance, while power politics techniques such as coercive threats or enforcement actions may help to contain or abate violence and facilitate negotiations, the parties must, sooner or later, be brought together at the negotiating table to try to iron out their differences. It is at this stage that the variants of the problem-solving approach can be fruitfully applied.

At present, the OAU and OAS tend to concentrate on controlling or abating conflicts, leaving the root causes of those conflicts untouched. To be able to sustain serious negotiations that explore those root causes and produce lasting solutions, both organisations need a mediatory organ. At the same time, they also need to enhance some of their control and abatement techniques, especially in the areas of peace-keeping and monitoring, to be able to bring the parties in conflict to the point of entering into meaningful negotiations. The development of confidence-building measures and integrative activities would also help to not only assist, in the restoration of peace, but also prevent the outbreak of conflicts in the first place.

All these improvements in the conflict management machinery and techniques employed by the OAU and OAS would not only guarantee peaceful and harmonious relations in either region, they would also significantly enhance the chances of preventing, controlling, and resolving the conflicts that continue to plague Africa and the Americas.

Notes

1. T.A. Imobighe (1989), *op. cit.*, pp. 45-47.
2. This was done at the 1992 Dakar Summit at the insistence of the then Secretary-General, Salim Ahmed Salim who, especially, between 1990 and 1993, intensely pushed for improvements in the OAU's conflict management mechanism.
3. OAS Document, *AG/RES. 1063 (XX-0/90)*, Resolution Adopted at the Eight Plenary Session held on June 8, 1990.
4. This was obvious from the cold reception given to the OAU Secretary-General, Salim Ahmed Salim's proposal on peace-keeping presented at the Dakar Summit in July 1992.
5. Salim Ahmed Salim, "The Price of Peace", in *The West African Bulletin*, No. 3, ECOWAS Executive Secretariat, Lagos, June 1995, p. 5.
6. This was at the Sixty-Second Ordinary Session of the Council of Ministers held in Addis Ababa, Ethiopia, from 20 to 28 June 1995.
7. *Annual Report of the Secretary-General, 1990-1991*, OEA Ser.O III-41 1990-91 End. (Washington, D.C.: OAS General Secretariat, 1990-91).
8. This information provided by OAU Secretary-General, Salim Ahmed Salim, to the author in a letter dated May 19, 1992.
9. *AHG/Dec.1 (XXVIII)*, Dakar, Senegal, 29 June to 1 July 1992.

Chapter 8

Conclusion:

Extra-Regional Dimension of Regional Conflict Management

WHAT has been done in this study is a critical assessment of the conflict management efforts of the OAU and OAS, within the framework of an integrated conflict management system. The study not only looks into the machinery the two regional organisations have put in place for the purpose of managing conflicts within their respective regions, but also the conflict management techniques they have adopted. It is observed that despite the fact that they operate from different geo-strategic setting, the machinery established by both the OAU and OAS do not show too much dissimilarities. Another important observation is the susceptibility of both regions to basically the same types of conflict, though the intensity of these conflicts may vary from one region to the other.

As for their conflict management methods, both organisations have relied more on conference diplomacy and ad hoc arrangements than the problem-solving techniques. Other techniques frequently used, especially by the OAS include investigative methods and coercive tactics. This is obviously because the OAS's interventions have often been carried out under the Rio Treaty, which is basically a collective defence arrangement against aggressive tendencies within the region.

Overall, the study documents the areas of strength and weaknesses of the two organisations and proffers some pertinent suggestions for optimising the conflict management performance of both organisations. There is no doubt that other IGOs, both regional and global, stand to benefit from the suggested measures. While the suggestions proffered in this study could considerably enhance the conflict management performances of the OAU and

OAS, it is clearly evident from this study that it takes more than the responses of the members of an IGO for it to be a successful conflict manager. In fact, this study has shown that the responses of non-member-states could equally be critical. Hence, this conclusive chapter is hinged on the subject title of the extra-regional dimension of regional conflict management.

The involvement of extra-regional states, interests, and groups in regional conflicts has compounded the problem of managing those conflicts. While this problem has been more acute in Africa than in the American hemisphere, it has also had a debilitating impact on the efforts of the OAS. This was particularly apparent during the Cold War, when the East-West rivalry often spread to Latin America, bringing the Soviet Union and the United States to give their support to opposing sides in Latin American conflicts. In Nicaragua, to take but one example, the United States supported the Contra rebels against the Soviet-backed Sandinista government.

The vulnerability of the OAU to extra-regional intervention is hard to overstate, given the fact that the organisation's entire membership, with perhaps the exception of South Africa, suffer from the basic problem of external dependency. The situation in Africa is such that the OAU easily loses control of conflicts when they escalate into open military hostilities, at which point the parties are bound to rely on external sources for the means of prosecuting the war. Among the many examples that might be cited are the conflicts between Somalia and Ethiopia, Uganda and Tanzania and even the Chadian civil war.

Effective management of a conflict by a regional organisation thus frequently depends not only on the responses of its members, but also on the behaviour of powers outside the region. This is one reason why conflict management, if it is to be successful, should involve IGOs from outside as well as inside the affected region. Co-operation among IGOs is also important for at least two other reasons. First, co-operation is necessary to promote the most efficient use of scarce resources. The acute shortage of resources for conflict management, especially in some of the less advanced regions of the world, suggests the need for resource input from the more advanced regions and a more reliable programme of resource mobilisation and conservation, as well as burden-sharing, between regional bodies and the United Nations.

Second, almost all states belong to the United Nations, as well as to regional bodies. Because of the lack of effective and well articulated routine co-operation between the world body and regional groups in the area of conflict management, some countries have hopped from one organisation to another, to ease or escape pressure on them to embark on serious negotiations to resolve their conflicts with other states. Morocco, for example, has used this tactic to stall the settlement of its dispute with Western Sahara. There have been a number of cases in which the United Nations and the OAS were involved in parallel actions on the same conflict, leading not only to the duplication of efforts but also, at times, to situations in which the two organisations were working at cross-purposes.[10]

The end of the cold war and the improved international system, however, has led to a greater awareness that collaboration between the UN and regional organisations can have salutary effect in peace-making and conflict resolution. Possible models of such collaboration to be encouraged, fine-tuned and built upon include the ASEAN/UN efforts which led to the Paris Conference on the Cambodian conflict; the UN/OAU/IOC/Arab League peace efforts in Somalia; and UN/European Community joint peace efforts in the territories of former Yugoslavia. Others include the "Friends of the Secretary-General" approach adopted in EI Salvador, where the UN took the leading role and supported by key states with influence in the region and adequate knowledge of the realities of the conflict situation; and the rather complex role played by some groups of states, the UN and OAS in bringing an end to the war in Nicaragua.

As the following brief discussions suggest, Inter-IGO cooperation[11] could usefully occur within all three stages of the conflict management circle.

Co-operation at the Conflict Prevention and Peace Promotion Stage

Possible organisational responses at this stage include the

establishment of behavioural codes, the creation of confidence-building measures, and the promotion of bilateral and multilateral integrative activities. Although the United Nations and regional organisations have laid down certain principles and rules of conduct in their charters and other instruments to promote peace and harmony at both the regional and global levels, compliance remains a problem. To ensure greater respect for their principles and rule, IGOs could encourage the setting up of similar behavioural codes and develop common rules of compliance with internationally accepted norms of behaviour. Thus, a state that has forfeited the right to interact with the members of an IGO in which it is a member because of its violation of an internationally recognised principle, should not be given any solace by any other IGO.

Providing greater opportunity for frequent contact in all areas of human endeavour at both the intra-organisational and inter-organisational levels is another way IGOs can help to promote global understanding. Movement in this direction could begin with more frequent contacts between the secretariat staff of these organisations, opening channels of communication for the exchange of information and the co-ordination of programs and activities. All regional organisations would stand to benefit from learning about each other's experiences in conflict management.

Co-operation at the Conflict Control and Abatement Stage

Depending on the level of escalation at which the conflict is being managed, organisational responses usually take the form of appeals to the parties involved to exercise restraint, imposition and enforcement of sanctions, and the use of peace-keeping, peace-monitoring and observation forces to separate opposing forces and supervise cease-fires. Inter-organisational co-operation in all these areas could be effected in a number of ways.

To begin with, parallel resolutions for restraint from both the United Nations and regional organisations will tend to boost the efforts of the organisation involved in the management of the conflict. If, however, it becomes necessary to impose sanctions to induce the parties to come to the negotiating table, inter-organisational co-operation becomes even more important. For their effectiveness, sanctions depend on widespread compliance. This cannot be achieved by a single regional organisation, for its resolutions are binding only on its own members, leaving other states free to continue to trade with the targeted member-state. Thus, for instance, the sanctions imposed by the OAS on Haiti, following the overthrow of President Aristide's government by the military, did nothing to stop Haiti importing and exporting goods to states outside the OAS. Again, OAU's sanctions against apartheid South Africa during the liberation struggle in that territory was weakened by the non-compliance, especially of some Western countries. Clearly, the success of sanctions would be greatly enhanced if they were to be imposed, or at least respected, by a majority of, if not all IGOs. Given its global character, the participation of the United Nations in any programme of sanctions would be vital.

Another area where co-operation is necessary is in peace-keeping. Since the 1950s, the United Nations has undertaken dozens of peace-keeping missions throughout the world, but its success in this endeavour has been mixed. Furthermore, since the end of the cold war, there has been an increasing demand for UN peace-keeping forces, a demand that is straining to breaking point the already over-extended resources of the world body. In 1992, for example, UN Secretary-General, Boutros Boutros-Ghali, noted that the organisation had approved "close to $3 billion" for peace-keeping operations in the current 12 month period, even while the UN's unpaid peace-keeping debt amounted to more than $800 million.[12] The time seems to have come for the United Nations to evolve a more cost-effective global strategy of peace-keeping that is centred on regional organisations.

Logistically, the mobilisation of peace-keeping forces could be accomplished more cost-effectively if the troops were deployed from the regions where the conflicts were to occur instead of being air-lifted or shipped from distant regions of the globe. Regional organisations could be encouraged to develop programmes for regular joint training and exercises of the armed forces of their member-states, thereby providing the United Nations with a nucleus of peace-keeping forces that are accustomed to working together. These forces would be likely to appreciate the climatic and geographical conditions in the areas of their deployment, and could be deployed rapidly.

To meet the expenses involved in these regular training exercises, every IGO will need to set up a special fund, call it "peace fund", to which members will contribute, under agreed mode of assessment. This could be augmented by possible voluntary contributions from other sources both within and outside the affected region.

While such inter-organisational co-operation would help to reduce the costs of peace-keeping and permit greater efficiency and more timely action to be taken to abate the conflict, the ultimate goal should be to use peace-keeping exercises to create an atmosphere conducive to serious negotiations. In other words, determined efforts should be made to reduce the length of peace-keeping operations through the aggressive pursuit of a peace settlement between the parties in conflict. As this study has illustrated, tardiness in following up peace-keeping activities with serious mediation has resulted in the unnecessary prolongation of a number of peace-keeping operations. Peace-keeping operations need to be seen as but one part of an integrated conflict management approach in which resolutions, sanctions, mediation, and conciliation are all employed as required in pursuit of an early resolution of the conflict.

Co-operation at the Conflict Resolution Stage

At the stage of conflict resolution, third parties need to exercise considerable patience and perseverance if they are to help the parties in conflict reach a lasting settlement. Unfortunately, most IGOs have only been casually disposed toward serious and sustained mediation. As this study has emphasised, IGOs have great need of a permanent mediation organ comprised of highly respected persons with the time, expertise, and inclination to facilitate and sustain the lengthy process of negotiation.

Inter-organisational co-operation at this stage could be effected by the use of joint mediation teams. For instance, if the OAU, the OAS, and the United Nations were to operate such an arrangement, each of the three organisations would provide one member of a three-person mediation team created to handle a particular conflict. The team would thus possess not only persons of great eminence and experience but also the combined moral weight of the three organisations involved. Parties to a conflict would find it difficult to defy such a combination, especially if the affected IGOs are prepared to support their joint diplomatic efforts with appropriate sanctions to check recalcitrant behaviour on the part of any of the parties in conflict as was done in Bosnia.

To strengthen this type of collaboration, frequent contact and the exchange of ideas among the staff of the mediation organs of the various IGOS needs to be encouraged. In other words, the mediation organs should be another channel of regular interaction among the various IGOs. They should hold regular joint seminars and workshops to share ideas about the latest techniques and trends in conflict management. They should also meet regularly to discuss potential hot-spots and develop their capacity to respond promptly to incipient conflicts.

Inter-organisational collaboration can help to create a global network through which IGOs can collectively manage conflict within and between states in an integrated manner. To be sure, this is not a prescription to prevent the outbreak or ensure the resolution of all, or even most conflicts. No amount of organisational reform could be expected to accomplish that goal in the face of such problems as bitter political rivalries, pronounced asymmetries of power, and serious shortages of resources. Unless such reform is undertaken, however, more conflicts will erupt and fewer will be resolved than need be. The OAU and OAS cannot realistically hope to put an end to intra-state and inter-state violence within their respective regions. However, if they replace their present ad hoc and piecemeal approaches to conflict management with a more carefully considered and integrated approach, they can realistically expect to do a better job than they have done in the past.

Notes

1. Louis B. Sohn, ed., *Cases on United Nations Law* (Brooklyn:

The foundation Press, Inc., 1967), pp. 1055-1071.

2. It should be noted that the United Nations and regional organisations have a wider basis for co-operation in conflict management than do different regional bodies. This is because almost all members of regional organisations are also members of the United Nations, whereas only a few members of regional organisations, especially within Africa and the Americas, belong to two or more such similar political organisations. In other words, the global reach of the United Nations is such that there can hardly be any conflict in which, at least, one of its members is not involved.

3. Boutros Boutros-Ghali, *An Agenda for Peace* (New York: United Nations, 1992), p. 28.

Selected Bibliography

Allsebrook, Mary, *Prototypes of Peacemaking: The First Forty Years of the United Nations* (Chicago & London: St. James Press, 1986).

Amate, C.O.C., *Inside the OAU: Pan-Africanism in Practice* (New York: St. Martin's Press, 1986).

Amoo, Samuel, Ghartey, "The OAU and African Conflicts: The Political and Institutional Dynamics of Regional Conflict Management", Ph.D. Dissertation, (St Johns Hopkins University, Baltimore, Maryland, 1989).

Andemicael, B., *The OAU and UN: Relations Between the Organisation of African Unity and the UN* (New York: Africana, 1976).

Assefa, H., *Mediation of Civil Wars: Approaches and Strategies - The Sudan Conflict* (Boulder, Colorado: Westview Press, 1987)

Ball, Margaret M., *The OAS in Transition* (Hurham: Duke U.P., 1969).

Bell, Carol, *The Conventions of Crisis: A Study in Diplomatic Management* (London: O.U.P., 1971).

Boulding, Kenneth, *Conflict and Defence: A General Theory* (New York & London: Harper & Row, 1962).

Boutros-Ghali, Boutros, *An Agenda for Peace* (New York: UN, 1992).

Burton, John W., *Deviance, Terrorism and War: The Process of Solving Unresolved Social and Political Problems* (New York: St. Martins, 1979).

Burton, John W., *Global Conflict: The Domestic Sources of International Crisis* (Brighton, Sussex: Wheatsheaf Books, 1984).

Burton, John W., *World Society* (Lanham: University Press of America, 1987).

Burton, John W., *Resolving Deep-Rooted Conflict: A Handbook* (Lanham: University Press of America, 1987).

Burton, John W., "On the Need for Conflict Provention", Occasional Paper 1, Centre for Conflict Analysis and Resolution, (George Mason University, Fairfax, September 1989).

Burton, John W., *Conflict: Resolution and Prevention* (New York: St Martins Press, 1990).

Byron, Jessica, *Regional Security in Latin America and Africa: the OAS and OAU in the Light of Contemporary Security* (1984).

Child, Jack, (ed.) *Regional Co-operation for Development and the Peaceful Settlement of Disputes in Latin America* (New York: Martinus Nijhoff for IPA, 1987).

Cohen, Raymond, *Negotiating Across Cultures: Communication Obstacles in International Diplomacy* (Washington DC: USIP Press, 1991).

CSCE, *Peaceful Settlements of Dispute in the CSCE Process,* A Report Prepared by the Staff of CSCE, August 1991.

Deng, Francis M. and Zartman, I. William, (eds.) *Conflict Resolution in Africa* (Washington DC: The Brookings Institute, 1991).

Dreier, John C., *The Organisation of American States and the Hemisphere Crisis* (New York: Harper & Row for Council on Foreign Relations, 1962).

El-Ayouty, Yessin, (ed.) *The Organisation of African Unity After Ten Years* (New York: Praeger, 1975).

El-Ayouty, Yessin and Zartman, I. William, (eds.) *The OAU After Twenty Years* (New York: Praeger, 1984).

Farer, Tom J., (ed.) *The Future of the Inter-American System* (New York: Praeger, 1979).

Fenwick, Dennis T., *The OAS and the Maintenance of Peace and Security: Trends* (Kent: Ohio, 1969).

Fraser, Niall M. and Hipel, Keith W., *Conflict Analysis, Models and Resolutions* (New York: Elseviep Science Publishing Co., 1984).

Fisher, Roger and Ury, William, *Getting to Yes: Negotiating Agreement Without Giving In* (New York: Penguin, 1983).

George, Alexander I., (ed.) *Avoiding War: Problems of Crisis Management* (Boulder: Westview Press, 1991).

George, Alexander I., *Forceful Persuasion, Coercive Diplomacy as an Alternative to War* (Washington DC: USIP Press, 1991).

Haas, Ernst B. et. al. *Conflict Management by International Organisations* (Morristown: General Learning Press, 1972).

Hassouna, Hussein A., *The League of Arab States and Regional Disputes* (New York: Oceana, 1975).

Imobighe, T.A., *The OAU, African Defence and Security* (Benin & Owerri: Adena, 1989).

Keltner, John W. (Sam), *Mediation: Towards A Civilized System of Dispute Resolution* (Urbana: Eric & SCA Publication, 1987).

Lauterpacht, E. Obe QC. et. al., (eds.) *The Kuwait Crisis: Basic Documents* (Cambridge: Grotius Publications, 1991).

Lewis, I. M., (ed.) *Nationalism and Self-Determination in the Horn of Africa* (London: Ithaca Press, 1983).

Liu, F.T., *United Nations Peace-keeping: Management and Operations* (New York: IPA, 1990).

Lowenthal, Abraham F., *Partners in Conflict: The United States and Latin America* (Baltimore: The Johns Hopkins U.P., 1987).

Macdonald, Robert W., *The League of Arab States: A Study in the Dynamics of Regional Organisations* (Princeton, New Jersey: P.U.P, 1965).

Miller, Nicola, *Soviet Relations With Latin America* (Cambridge & New York: Cambridge U.P., 1989).

Mills, Susan R., *The Financing of United Nations Peace-keeping Operations: The Need for a Sound Financial Basis* (New York: IPA, 1989).

Mitchell, C.R. and Webb, K., (eds.) *New Approaches to International Mediation* (New York: Greenwood Press, 1989).

Moore, Christopher W., *The Mediation Process: Practical Strategies for Resolving Conflict* (San Francisco & London: Jossey-Bass, 1987).

Morris, Michael A. and Milan, Victor, (eds.) *Controlling Latin American Conflicts: Ten Approaches* (Boulder: Westview Press, 1983).

OAS Association, *The OAS: The Quiet Force Defending Democracy and Progress,* (Washington DC: 1968).

Obaseki, Nosakhare O. (ed.) *Africa and the Super-Powers: External Involvement in Regional Disputes* (New York: IPA Report, No. 14 1983).

Obaseki, Nosakhare O., *Managing Africa's Conflicts* (New York: IPA Report, No. 12 1982).

Pruitt, Dean G., *Social Conflict, Escalation, Stalemate and Settlement* (New York: Random House, 1986).

Ruben, Jeffrey Z., (ed.) *Dynamics of Third-Party Intervention* (New York: Praeger, 1981).

Sandole, Dennis J.D. and Sandole-Staroste, Ingrid, (eds.) *Conflict Management and Problem-Solving: Interpersonal to International Applications* (New York: N.Y. University Press, 1987).

Scheman, L. Ronald, *The Inter-American Dilemma* (New York: Praeger, 1988).

Sesay, Amadou et. al., *The OAU After Twenty Years* (Boulder: Westview Press, 1984).

Skidmore, Thomas E. and Smith, Peter H., *Modern Latin America,* Second edition (New York: O.U.P., 1989).

Slater, Jerome, *The OAS and UN Policy* (Ohio: State University Press, 1967).

Stremlau, John J., *The International Politics of the Nigerian Civil War, 1967-1970* (Princeton, New Jersey: Princeton U.P., 1977).

Touval, Saadia, *The Peace Brokers: Mediation in the Arab-Israeli Conflict, 1948-79* (Princeton: O.U.P., 1982).

Touval, Saadia, *The Boundary Politics of Independent Africa* (Cambridge, Massachusetts: Harvard U.P., 1972).

Touval, Saadia and Zartman, I William, (eds.) *International Mediation in Theory and Practice* (Boulder: Westview Press, 1985).

Wainhouse, David W., *International Peace Observation* (Baltimore: The Johns Hopkins Press, 1966).

Wiseman, Henry, (ed.) *Peace-keeping: Appraisals and Proposals* (New York: Pergamon Press, 1983).

Zacher, Mark W., *International Conflicts and Collective Security, 1946-77* (New York: Praeger, 1979).

Zartman, I William, *Ripe for Resolution: Conflict and Intervention in Africa* (New York: O.U.P., 1985).

Appendix

The Hybrid Nature of Inter-state Disputes/ Conflicts in Africa and the Americas, 1899-1989

KEY

A = Boundary/territorial conflict
B = System/ideological conflict
C = Resource conflict
D = Hegemonic/influence Conflict
E = Migration/refugee conflict

AFRICA

	Conflicts	Date (from)	A	B	C	D	E
1.	Algeria – Morocco	1965	+	+	+	-	-
2.	Angola – Zaire	1977	+	+	+	-	+
3.	Benin - Nigeria	1981	+	-	-	-	-
4.	Benin (Dahomey) – Niger	1963	+	-	+	-	+
5.	Burundi – Rwanda	1964	-	+	-	-	+
6.	Cameroon – Nigeria	1961	+	-	+	-	-
7.	Chad – Niger	1972	+	-	+	-	-
8.	Chad – Libya	1973	+	-	+	-	-
9.	Chad – Sudan	1980	-	-	-	-	+
10.	Congo – Gabon	1962	+	-	+	-	-
11.	Congo – Zaire	1963	-	+	-	-	+
12.	Egypt – Sudan	1958	+	-	-	+	-
13.	Egypt – Libya	1977	+	+	-	-	-
14.	Ethiopia – Somalia	1963	+	-	-	-	-

15.	Ethiopia – Eritrea	1962	+	-	-	+	-
16.	Ghana – Togo	1958	+	+	-	-	+
17.	Ghana – Ivory Cost	1959	-	+	-	-	+
18.	Ghana – Niger	1965	-	+	-	-	+
19.	Ghana – Upper Volta (Burkina Faso)	1963	+	+	-	-	+
20.	Ghana – Guinea	1966	-	+	-	-	+
21.	Guinea – Ivory Cost	1966	-	+	-	-	+
22.	Guinea – Senegal	1971	+	+	-	-	-
23.	Guinea Bissau – Senegal	1978	+	-	-	-	-
24.	Gabon – Cameroon	1960	+	-	-	-	-
25.	Gabon – Equatorial Guinea	1967	+	-	-	-	-
26.	Kenya – Somalia	1963	+	-	-	-	-
27.	Kenya – Tanzania	1977	-	+	-	-	+
28.	Kenya – Uganda	1976	+	-	-	-	-
29.	Lesotho – South Africa	1966	+	-	-	-	-
30.	Libya – Tunisia	1975	+	-	-	-	-
31.	Libya – Tunisia	1980	+	+	-	-	-
32.	Mali – Burkina Faso	1975	+	-	-	-	-
33.	Mali – Mauritania	1960	+	-	-	-	-
34.	Malawi – Tanzania	1967	+	+	-	-	+
35.	Malawi – Zambia	1967	+	+	-	-	-
36.	Mauritania – Morocco	1956	+	-	-	+	-
37.	Mauritania – Senegal	1989	+	-	-	-	-
38.	Morocco – Mali	1963	+	-	-	-	-
39.	Morocco – Western Sahara	1972	+	-	-	+	-
40.	Sudan – Ethiopia	1965	-	-	-	-	+
41.	Sudan – Kenya	1963	+	-	+	-	-
42.	Sudan – Uganda	1978	-	-	-	-	+
43.	Tunisia – Algeria	1956	+	-	-	-	-
44.	Uganda – Tanzania	1972	+	+	-	-	-

45.	Zaire Vs Zambia	1977	+	+	-	-	-

THE AMERICAS

	Conflicts	Date (from)	A	B	C	D	E
1.	Argentina – Brazil	1952	-	-	+	+	-
2.	Argentina – Chile	1948	+	-	+	+	+
3.	Argentina – Paraguay	1964	-	-	+	+	+
4.	Argentina – Uruguay	1963	+	-	-	+	+
5.	Belize – Guatemala	1972	+	-	-	+	-
6.	Bolivia – Brazil	1903	-	-	+	-	+
7.	Bolivia – Chile	1962	+	-	+	-	-
8.	Bolivia – Paraguay	1932	+	+	-	-	-
9.	Bolivia – Peru	1964	+	-	+	-	+
10.	Brazil – Guyana	1976	+	-	+	+	-
11.	Brazil – Paraguay	1962	-	-	+	+	-
12.	Chile – Cuba	1964	-	+	-	-	-
13.	Chile – Peru	1972	+	-	+	-	-
14.	Colombia – Nicaragua	1979	+	+	-	-	-
15.	Colombia – Venezuela	1966	+	-	+	-	+
16.	Costa Rica – Cuba	1960	-	+	-	-	-
17.	Costa Rica – Nicaragua	1948	+	+	-	-	+
18.	Cuba – Honduras	1964	-	+	-	-	-
19.	Cuba – United States	1960	+	+	-	+	+
20.	Dominica Republic – Haiti	1949	+	+	-	+	+
21.	Ecuador – Peru	1945	+	-	+	-	-
22.	El Salvador – Cuba	1979	+	+	-	-	-
23.	El Salvador – Honduras	1967	+	-	+	-	+
24.	El Salvador – Nicaragua	1979	+	+	-	-	-
25.	Guatemala – Cuba	1964	-	+	-	-	-
26.	Guyana – Suriname	1969	+	+	+	-	-
27.	Haiti – United States	1991	-	-	-	+	+
28.	Honduras – Nicaragua	1957	+	+	-	-	+

29.	Jamaica – Cuba	1981	-	+	-	-	-
30.	Mexico – United States	1945	+	+	+	+	+
31.	Nicaragua – United States	1980	-	+	-	+	-
32.	Panama – United States	1946	+	+	+	+	-
33.	Trinidad & Tobago – Venezuela	1975	+	-	+	+	-
34.	Venezuela – Guyana	1899	+	-	+	+	-

Note: The above list is not exhaustive, and is chiefly meant to illustrate the hybrid nature of most of the conflicts in Africa and the Americas, and thus, to highlight the problem inherent in trying to classify them under one typology.

Index

www.ingramcontent.com/pod-product-compliance
Ingram Content Group UK Ltd.
Pitfield, Milton Keynes, MK11 3LW, UK
UKHW020123290926
15471UKWH00003B/250

9 789780 293741